THE SIMPLE 5-INGREDIENT LOW-CARB HIGH-PROTEIN COOKBOOK

Quick & Easy Fat-Burning Meals for Busy People Looking to Lose Weight — Includes 100+ Recipes, a 30-Day Meal Plan, and Shopping Lists

By Dolores Abrams

Published by Kwon Royalty Publishing, under its Tasty Shelf imprint.

All recipes in this cookbook were tested and enjoyed by chefs and home cooks to ensure quality, simplicity, and real results.

GET YOUR FREE EXCLUSIVE BONUSES NOW!

Download for Free – Simply Scan the QR Code Below!

30-DAY MEAL PLAN

SHOPPING LIST

MEDITERRANEAN DIET RECIPE E-BOOK

Contents

Drinks..83

Desserts 94

30 Day Meal Plan and Shopping list 105

WHAT IS A LOW-CARB, HIGH-PROTEIN DIET?

A low-carb, high-protein diet is a smart, sustainable approach to eating that focuses on reducing your intake of carbohydrates—like bread, pasta, rice, sugar, and starchy foodswhile increasing your intake of protein-rich whole foods such as lean meats, eggs, fish, dairy, and tofu. The goal is to shift the body's primary energy source from carbohydrates to fat, while giving your body the protein it needs to build and repair tissues, maintain muscle, and keep you feeling satisfied throughout the day.

Protein is a vital macronutrient that plays an essential role in nearly every function of the body. When paired with a reduction in carbs, this diet can support fat burning without muscle loss, promote more stable energy levels, and reduce frequent hunger spikes. Unlike diets that require severe calorie restriction or eliminate entire food groups, a low-carb, high-protein approach is all about balance, simplicity, and fueling your body the right way.

Main Benefits of a Low-Carb, High-Protein Diet:

Weight Loss – Helps burn fat without sacrificing muscle mass.
Metabolism Boost – Encourages lean muscle development, which helps burn more calories.
Muscle Maintenance – Provides the essential amino acids your body needs for recovery and strength.
Appetite Control – Keeps you fuller longer and reduces sugar cravings.
Blood Sugar Regulation – Prevents energy crashes by stabilizing glucose levels throughout the day.

Who Is This Diet For?

This diet is perfect for beginners and for those who want to eat healthy without feeling overwhelmed. Whether you're trying to lose weight, maintain muscle, or simply feel better in your everyday life, this way of eating offers a realistic and flexible foundation. You don't need to be a chef or a nutritionist—just someone looking for easy, delicious meals that fit into a busy lifestyle. If you're looking for a clear, step-by-step solution to better health with real, satisfying food, this cookbook is made for you.

WHY THIS COOKBOOK?

In a world filled with fad diets, complicated meal plans, and endless nutrition advice, it's easy to feel overwhelmed. That's why this cookbook was created—to bring clarity, simplicity, and real results into your kitchen. Whether you're just beginning your health journey or looking for a more practical way to stay consistent, this book is your step-by-step guide to clean, low-carb, high-protein eating that's both easy and enjoyable.

What sets this cookbook apart is its emphasis on simplicity. Every recipe is made with just 5 main ingredients or fewer, so you can spend less time shopping, prepping, and cooking—and more time enjoying food that supports your health goals. These meals are quick and satisfying, perfect for busy mornings, work lunches, and effortless weeknight dinners. But this book isn't about extreme dieting or cutting out everything you love. It's about balance and sustainability. You'll enjoy real food that fuels your body, keeps you full, and helps you build habits that last. No complex calorie counting. No guilt. Just simple meals that work.

After struggling with her own health and weight challenges, chef Dolores Abrams transformed her life by embracing a low-carb, high-protein lifestyle—without the overwhelm. This cookbook reflects that journey and is here to help you do the same.

Inside, you'll find 100+ low-carb, high-protein recipes made with just 5 ingredients or fewer, plus a 30-day meal plan, shopping lists, and full nutritional breakdowns—including macros—to help you stay on track with ease.

BREAKFAST

AVOCADO & EGG PROTEIN BOWL

PREP TIME

05 MINS

COOK TIME

7 MINS

SERVINGS

1

INGREDIENTS

- 2 large eggs
- ½ avocado, sliced
- 1 oz feta cheese (or cheddar)
- 1 tsp olive oil
- Salt & black pepper (to taste)

INSTRUCTIONS

1. Preheat a non-stick skillet on moderate heat and drizzle in olive oil.
2. Crack the eggs, throw them into the pan, and cook to your preferred doneness—fried or over-easy, which works great here.
3. While the eggs cook, slice the avocado and crumble the cheese.
4. Arrange the avocado slices in a deep-bottom bowl.
5. Add the eggs over the avocado, sprinkle with cheese, and powder it with salt and crushed pepper.
6. Serve warm as a nourishing, protein-rich breakfast.

NUTRITIONAL VALUES (PER SERVING):

Calories: 330 | Fat: 27g | Cholesterol: 372mg | Total Carbohydrates: 6.7g | Sugar: 0.8g | Protein: 21g | Sodium: 350mg | Fiber: 5g

Refrigeration:
Best served fresh.

Reheating:
Warm eggs separately if needed. Avocado is best added fresh.

KETO COTTAGE CHEESE PANCAKES (HIGH-PROTEIN)

PREP TIME

05 MINS

COOK TIME

10 MINS

SERVINGS

1

INGREDIENTS

- 2 large eggs
- ¾ cup full-fat cottage cheese
- 2 tbsp almond flour
- Pinch of salt

NUTRITIONAL VALUES (PER SERVING):

Calories: 370 | Fat: 23g | Cholesterol: 410mg | Total Carbohydrates: 6.9g | Sugar: 2.4g | Protein: 32g | Sodium: 600mg | Fiber: 1.5g

Refrigeration:
Store in an air-sealed container for up to 2 days.

Reheating:
Microwave for 30–45 seconds or warm in a skillet.

INSTRUCTIONS

1. Add eggs, cottage cheese, almond flour, and salt into a bowl.
2. Mix thoroughly until well combined. The texture will be thick but pourable.
3. Preheat a non-stick skillet on moderate heat.
4. Spoon about two tbsp batter for one pancake onto the skillet.
5. Cook both sides for 2–3 minutes until golden and firm in the center.
6. Plate and enjoy warm. These pair well with a dollop of almond butter or Greek yogurt if desired.

GROUND TURKEY & EGG SCRAMBLE

PREP TIME

05 MINS

COOK TIME

6 MINS

SERVINGS

1

NUTRITIONAL VALUES (PER SERVING):

Calories: 315 | Fat: 24.2g | Cholesterol: 390mg | Total Carbohydrates: 1.7g | Sugar: 0.3g | Protein: 25.5g | Sodium: 480mg | Fiber: 0g

Refrigeration:
Store in an airtight container for up to 2 days.

Reheating:
Warm gently in a skillet or microwave for 30–45 seconds.

INGREDIENTS

- 2 large eggs
- 2 oz ground turkey lean ground turkey
- 2 tbsp shredded cheddar cheese
- 1 tbsp olive oil
- Salt & black pepper (to taste)

INSTRUCTIONS

1. Heat olive oil in a skillet on moderate heat. Add the ground turkey and cook for 4–5 minutes, breaking it apart with a spatula, until no longer pink.
2. While the turkey is cooking, whisk the eggs in a bowl with salt and pepper.
3. Pour the eggs over the cooked turkey and gently scramble until just set.
4. Sprinkle the cheddar cheese on top and let it melt for 1 minute before serving hot.

LOW-CARB SAUSAGE MUFFINS (HIGH-PROTEIN)

PREP TIME
05 MINS

COOK TIME
15 MINS

SERVINGS
2

INGREDIENTS

- 2 large eggs
- 3 oz ground sausage
- 2 tbsp almond flour
- ¼ cup shredded cheddar cheese
- Salt & pepper (to taste)

NUTRITIONAL VALUES (PER SERVING):

Calories: 290 | Fat: 23g | Cholesterol: 240mg | Total Carbohydrates: 2.8g | Sugar: 0.6g | Protein: 22g | Sodium: 460mg | Fiber: 1.5g

Refrigeration:
Store in a air-sealed container for up to 3 days.

Reheating:
Microwave for 30–40 seconds or reheat in the oven.

INSTRUCTIONS

1. Preheat oven to 375°F (190°C). Grease a muffin tin.
2. Grab the shallow bowl and combine eggs, raw sausage, almond flour, cheese, salt, and crushed pepper.
3. Mix well and spoon evenly into 2 muffin cups.
4. Bake for 15 minutes until the upper surface is golden and centers are cooked through.
5. Let them cool slightly, then serve warm.

PROTEIN CHIA PUDDING WITH ALMOND BUTTER & WHEY

PREP TIME
05 MINS

COOK TIME
00 MINS

SERVINGS
1

INGREDIENTS

- 2 tbsp chia seeds
- 1 tbsp almond butter
- ½ cup unsweetened almond milk
- 1 scoop vanilla or unflavored whey protein isolate
- Optional: a dash of ground cinnamon or vanilla extract

NUTRITIONAL VALUES (PER SERVING):

Calories: 290 | Fat: 16g | Cholesterol: 30mg | Total Carbohydrates: 6.3g | Sugar: 1g | Protein: 22g | Sodium: 75mg | Fiber: 9g

Refrigeration:
Store for up to 3 days in a sealed container.

Reheating:
Best enjoyed cold or at room temperature.

INSTRUCTIONS

1. Combine the chia seeds, almond butter, almond milk, and whey protein in a wide-mouth jar or deep-bottom bowl.
2. Stir thoroughly to prevent clumping. Let it sit for 5 minutes, stir again, then chill for 2 hours (at least) or overnight.
3. Stir once more before eating. Enjoy cold as a creamy, protein-packed breakfast.

SPINACH & FETA EGG SCRAMBLE

PREP TIME

05 MINS

COOK TIME

7 MINS

SERVINGS

1

INGREDIENTS

- 2 large eggs
- 1 cup cooked spinach
- 1 oz feta cheese
- 1 tbsp olive oil
- Salt & pepper (to taste)

NUTRITIONAL VALUES (PER SERVING):

Calories: 375 | Fat: 30g | Cholesterol: 397mg | Total Carbohydrates: 9.1g | Sugar: 2.6g | Protein: 21.3g | Sodium: 566mg | Fiber: 4.3g

Refrigeration:
Store for up to 2 days in an airtight container.

Reheating:
Microwave for 45 seconds or reheat on a skillet.

INSTRUCTIONS

1. Preheat a skillet on moderate heat and add olive oil.
2. Add cooked spinach to the skillet and sauté for 1 minute.
3. Grab the shallow bowl and beat the eggs with salt (just a pinch) and crushed pepper.
4. Pour the eggs into the skillet softly and gently scramble with the spinach.
5. Once nearly set, crumble in the feta and continue cooking for another minute.
6. Serve warm and enjoy your savory high-protein start.

SAVORY TOFU SCRAMBLE

PREP TIME

05 MINS

COOK TIME

8 MINS

SERVINGS

1

INGREDIENTS

- 6 oz firm tofu, drained and crumbled
- 1 tbsp olive oil (or avocado oil)
- ¼ cup chopped bell pepper
- ¼ cup chopped spinach
- 2 tbsp nutritional yeast
- Salt & black pepper (to taste)

NUTRITIONAL VALUES (PER SERVING):

Calories: 282 | Fat: 20.1g | Cholesterol: 0mg | Total Carbohydrates: 5.2g | Sugar: 1.1g | Protein: 22.4g | Sodium: 160mg | Fiber: 2.1g

Refrigeration:
Store in a sealed container for up to 2 days.

Reheating:
Rewarm in a skillet for 2–3 minutes or microwave for 1 minute.

INSTRUCTIONS

1. Heat olive oil in a nonstick skillet on moderate heat. Add crumbled tofu and cook for 3–4 minutes, allowing moisture to evaporate and light browning to begin.
2. Add bell pepper and spinach. Cook for another 3–4 minutes, stirring occasionally, until vegetables soften.
3. Stir in nutritional yeast, salt, and pepper. Toss everything together and cook for 1 more minute until well mixed and heated through.
4. Serve hot as a savory, protein-packed start to your day.

KETO GREEK YOGURT PARFAIT

PREP TIME	COOK TIME	SERVINGS
05 MINS	00 MINS	1

INGREDIENTS

- ¾ cup plain Greek yogurt
- 1 scoop vanilla or unflavored whey protein isolate
- 1 oz crumbled feta cheese (optional savory twist)

NUTRITIONAL VALUES (PER SERVING):

Calories: 285 | Fat: 7.5g | Cholesterol: 65mg | Total Carbohydrates: 9.2g | Sugar: 7g | Protein: 42g | Sodium: 405mg | Fiber: 0g

Refrigeration:
Store in a sealed container for 1 day.

Reheating:
Not required. Best served cold.

INSTRUCTIONS

1. Grab the shallow bowl and mix the Greek yogurt and whey protein until fully combined.
2. Layer into a parfait glass (use wide-mouth) or bowl.
3. Optionally, sprinkle with crumbled feta for a salty contrast.
4. Serve chilled.

FLAXSEED PROTEIN SMOOTHIE

PREP TIME

05 MINS

COOK TIME

00 MINS

SERVINGS

1

INGREDIENTS

- 1 scoop whey protein (vanilla or unflavored)
- 1 tbsp ground flaxseed
- 1 tbsp olive oil
- ½ cup cold water or unsweetened almond milk

NUTRITIONAL VALUES (PER SERVING):

Calories: 266 | Fat: 18g | Cholesterol: 30mg | Total Carbohydrates: 4g | Sugar: 1.2g | Protein: 21.3g | Sodium: 53mg | Fiber: 1.9g

Refrigeration:
Best consumed immediately.

Reheating:
Not applicable.

INSTRUCTIONS

1. Throw all ingredients into the powerful food blender.
2. Blend on full power for 30–45 seconds until their texture turns creamy and smooth.
3. Pour into the tall glass and drink immediately for a quick protein hit.

CAULIFLOWER HASH BROWN & EGG STACK

PREP TIME
10MINS

COOK TIME
10 MINS

SERVINGS
1

NUTRITIONAL VALUES (PER SERVING):

Calories: 380 | Fat: 29.6g | Cholesterol: 397mg | Total Carbohydrates: 4.9g | Sugar: 3.4g | Protein: 24.5g | Sodium: 456mg | Fiber: 1.3g

Refrigeration:
Store components separately for 2 days.

Reheating:
Reheat patty in skillet; cook egg fresh if possible.

INGREDIENTS

- ½ cup grated cauliflower
- 2 large eggs
- 1 oz feta cheese
- 1 scoop unflavored whey protein
- 1 tbsp olive oil

INSTRUCTIONS

1. Grab the shallow bowl and combine grated cauliflower, feta, and whey protein.
2. Heat one tbsp oil in a skillet on moderate heat.
3. Shape the cauliflower mixture into a patty and cook for 3–4 minutes on one side until golden.
4. Use the other pan to fry or poach the eggs to your liking. Stack the eggs over the hash browns and serve warm.

ALMOND BUTTER PROTEIN MUFFINS

PREP TIME

05 MINS

COOK TIME

12 MINS

SERVINGS

2

INGREDIENTS

- 1 tbsp almond butter (for nut-free, use sunflower seed butter)
- 1 large egg
- 1 scoop whey protein powder
- 2 tbsp almond flour (for nut-free, use sunflower seed flour)
- Pinch of salt

INSTRUCTIONS

1. Preheat oven to 350°F (175°C). Arrange the 2 muffin cups with paper liners.
2. Take the deep-bottom bowl and whisk together almond butter, egg, whey protein, almond flour, and salt until smooth.
3. Ladle the batter evenly into each muffin cup. Bake for 12 minutes until a toothpick is inserted and comes out clean.
4. Put them aside to sit for 5 minutes before serving.

NUTRITIONAL VALUES (PER SERVING):

Calories: 179 | Fat: 11.2g | Cholesterol: 108mg | Total Carbohydrates: 4.5g | Sugar: 1.4g | Protein: 16.2g | Sodium: 61mg | Fiber: 1.5g

Refrigeration:
Store in an air-sealed container for up to 3 days.

Reheating:
Microwave for 15–20 seconds.

ZUCCHINI & EGG FRITTATA

PREP TIME

7 MINS

COOK TIME

10 MINS

SERVINGS

3

INGREDIENTS

- 2 large eggs
- ½ cup shredded zucchini
- 1 oz feta cheese (for dairy-free, use lactose-free feta or goat cheese)
- 1 tbsp olive oil (can substitute avocado oil)
- Salt & pepper (to taste)

NUTRITIONAL VALUES (PER SERVING):

Calories: 115 | Fat: 9.9g | Cholesterol: 132mg | Total Carbohydrates: 1.5g | Sugar: 1.2g | Protein: 5.6g | Sodium: 148mg | Fiber: 0.2g

Refrigeration:
Store for up to 3 days.

Reheating:
Microwave for 30–45 seconds or reheat in oven at 300°F.

INSTRUCTIONS

1. Preheat oven to 375°F (190°C). Grease a small oven-safe dish.
2. On moderate heat, drizzle one tbsp oil into a skillet and toss in zucchini. Sauté for 2–3 minutes until softened.
3. Beat eggs in a deep-bottom bowl, then add sautéed zucchini, feta, salt, and crushed pepper.
4. Ladle the mixture into your prepared dish.
5. Bake for 10–12 minutes until golden and set. Put it aside to sit 3 minutes before slicing and serving.

TURKEY BACON EGG CUPS

PREP TIME	COOK TIME	SERVINGS
05 MINS	15 MINS	2

NUTRITIONAL VALUES (PER SERVING):

Calories: 163 | Fat: 11.7g | Cholesterol: 216mg | Total Carbohydrates: 1.1g | Sugar: 0.7g | Protein: 12.5g | Sodium: 300mg | Fiber: 0g

Refrigeration:
Store in an air-sealed container for up to 2 days.

Reheating:
Microwave for 20–30 seconds.

INGREDIENTS

- 2 large eggs
- 2 slices turkey bacon
- 1 oz cheddar cheese (for dairy-free, use dairy-free high-protein cheddar alternative)
- Salt & black pepper (to taste)

INSTRUCTIONS

1. Preheat oven to 375°F (190°C). Lightly grease two muffin cups.
2. Gently press one slice of turkey bacon into each muffin cup to form a shell.
3. Grab the shallow bowl, beat the eggs, and toss in shredded cheddar, salt, and crushed pepper.
4. Ladle the mixture into each cup.
5. Bake for 13-15 minutes until set and lightly browned. Let rest 2 minutes before serving.

KETO CHIA YOGURT BOWL

PREP TIME

5 MINS

COOK TIME

00 MINS

SERVINGS

1

INGREDIENTS

- 2 tbsp chia seeds
- ½ cup plain Greek yogurt (for dairy-free, use lactose-free high-protein Greek-style yogurt)
- 1 scoop vanilla or unflavored whey protein isolate (can be replaced with casein or beef protein)

NUTRITIONAL VALUES (PER SERVING):

Calories: 296 | Fat: 8.8g | Cholesterol: 35mg | Total Carbohydrates: 15g | Sugar: 3.7g | Protein: 35g | Sodium: 90mg | Fiber: 8g

Refrigeration:
Store in an air-sealed container for up to 2 days.

Reheating:
Not needed; best served cold.

INSTRUCTIONS

1. In a deep bowl, mix Greek yogurt and whey protein until smooth.
2. Toss in chia seeds and stir again to combine.
3. Let it sit for 5 minutes, stir once more, and chill for 1 hour to thicken.
4. Serve chilled with a spoon.

SCRAMBLED EGGS WITH PESTO

PREP TIME

3 MINS

COOK TIME

5 MINS

SERVINGS

1

INGREDIENTS

- 4 large eggs
- 1 tbsp pesto (for dairy-free, use dairy-free pesto)
- 1 tbsp olive oil (or avocado oil)
- Black pepper (to taste)

NUTRITIONAL VALUES (PER SERVING):

Calories: 391 | Fat: 32g | Cholesterol: 377mg | Total Carbohydrates: 2.2g | Sugar: 1.4g | Protein: 26g | Sodium: 280mg | Fiber: 0g

Refrigeration:
Store in a air-sealed container for up to 1 day.

Reheating:
Microwave for 30 seconds or warm gently in a skillet.

INSTRUCTIONS

1. Crack the eggs, and throw them into the bowl and beat until fluffy.
2. Massage in pesto and a pinch of black pepper.
3. Warm a skillet on moderate heat and add olive oil.
4. Ladle the egg mixture into the skillet and slowly scramble, moving in soft figure-eight motions.
5. Cook more for 2–3 minutes until set, then serve with extra pesto drizzled if desired.

VANILLA ALMOND PROTEIN SHAKE

PREP TIME
03 MINS

COOK TIME
00 MINS

SERVINGS
1

INGREDIENTS

- 1 cup unsweetened almond milk (for nut-free, use hemp or flax milk)
- 1 scoop + ½ scoop vanilla whey protein isolate (for a higher protein boost)
- 1 tbsp almond butter (for nut-free, use sunflower seed butter)

INSTRUCTIONS

1. Add almond milk, protein powder, and almond butter to the powerful food blender.
2. Blend on full power for 30 seconds until the texture gets smooth and creamy.
3. Let it sit for 1–2 minutes to thicken slightly. Serve chilled or over ice.

NUTRITIONAL VALUES (PER SERVING):

Calories: 293 | Fat: 13.8g | Cholesterol: 45mg | Total Carbohydrates: 7.3g | Sugar: 2.2g | Protein: 34.4g | Sodium: 236mg | Fiber: 1.6g

Refrigeration:
Store in a sealed jar for up to 1 day.

Reheating:
Not needed.

SAVORY TOFU BREAKFAST WRAP

PREP TIME
05 MINS

COOK TIME
07 MINS

SERVINGS
2

INGREDIENTS

- 3 oz firm tofu, crumbled
- 2 large eggs
- 1 medium low-carb tortilla (for gluten-free, use almond or coconut flour tortilla)
- 1 tbsp olive oil (or avocado oil)

NUTRITIONAL VALUES (PER SERVING):

Calories: 409 | Fat: 31.5g | Cholesterol: 372mg | Total Carbohydrates: 8.2g | Sugar: 2.6g | Protein: 26g | Sodium: 330mg | Fiber: 5g

Refrigeration:
Store filling separately for up to 2 days.

Reheating:
Microwave or reheat on skillet.

INSTRUCTIONS

1. Warm a skillet with one tbsp oil on moderate heat. Toss in tofu and cook for 2–3 minutes until golden.
2. Crack both eggs into the pan and scramble with tofu until cooked thoroughly. Warm the tortilla, fill it with the tofu-egg mix, and roll it tightly.
3. Serve hot.

MUSHROOM & HERB OMELET

PREP TIME

04 MINS

COOK TIME

06 MINS

SERVINGS

1

INGREDIENTS

- 3 large eggs
- ½ cup sliced mushrooms
- 1 tbsp chopped fresh herbs (parsley, chives, dill)
- 1 tbsp olive oil (or avocado oil)

NUTRITIONAL VALUES (PER SERVING):

Calories: 340 | Fat: 29g | Cholesterol: 558mg | Total Carbohydrates: 3.5g | Sugar: 2.3g | Protein: 19.1g | Sodium: 211mg | Fiber: 0.6g

Refrigeration:
Store for up to 1 day.

Reheating:
Warm in a pan or microwave.

INSTRUCTIONS

1. Heat a non-stick skillet on moderate heat with one tbsp oil. Toss in mushrooms and cook for 2–3 minutes.
2. Beat eggs and mix in herbs. Ladle into the pan and let set undisturbed for 2 minutes.
3. Fold gently and cook more for 1 minute. Let it sit before plating.

COCONUT CREAM CHIA BOWL

PREP TIME

05 MINS

COOK TIME

00 MINS

SERVINGS

1

INGREDIENTS

- ½ cup canned coconut milk (use light coconut milk for reduced fat)
- 2 tbsp chia seeds
- 1½ scoops vanilla whey protein isolate

NUTRITIONAL VALUES (PER SERVING):

Calories: 485 | Fat: 31.3g | Cholesterol: 45mg | Total Carbohydrates: 15g | Sugar: 2.5g | Protein: 37g | Sodium: 95mg | Fiber: 8g

Refrigeration:
Store in a air-sealed container for up to 2 days.

Reheating:
Not needed.

INSTRUCTIONS

1. Grab the shallow bowl and mix coconut milk and protein powder until smooth. Stir in chia seeds thoroughly.
2. Let it sit for 5 minutes, stir again, then cover and chill for 1 hour. Serve chilled.

EGGS IN AVOCADO BOATS

PREP TIME

05 MINS

COOK TIME

12 MINS

SERVINGS

2

INGREDIENTS

- 3 large eggs
- ½ medium avocado
- 1 tbsp olive oil (or avocado oil)
- Salt & black pepper (to taste)

NUTRITIONAL VALUES (PER SERVING):

Calories: 449 | Fat: 40g | Cholesterol: 558mg | Total Carbohydrates: 7.8g | Sugar: 2g | Protein: 21.5g | Sodium: 215mg | Fiber: 5g

Refrigeration:
Best eaten fresh. It can be kept up to 12 hours.

Reheating:
This dish is best enjoyed fresh. Reheating is not recommended, as the avocado may become watery and the eggs rubbery. If needed, enjoy leftovers cold or gently warmed in the microwave for 20–30 seconds.

INSTRUCTIONS

1. Cut the avocado in half and scoop a little more out to deepen the hole. Preheat oven to 375°F (190°C). Arrange the baking tray with parchment paper.
2. Carefully crack 1½ eggs into each half (you may discard a bit of white if needed). Drizzle with one tbsp oil, then sprinkle salt and crushed pepper.
3. Bake for 12 minutes until whites are firm and yolks soft. Let it sit 2 minutes before eating.

LUNCH

STUFFED BELL PEPPERS WITH GROUND TURKEY

PREP TIME 05 MINS | **COOK TIME** 20 MINS | **SERVINGS** 2

INGREDIENTS

- 2 medium bell peppers, halved and seeded (for lower carb, use green bell peppers)
- 8 oz ground turkey
- ¼ cup shredded cheddar cheese (for dairy-free, use dairy-free cheddar alternative)
- Salt & black pepper (to taste)

NUTRITIONAL VALUES (PER SERVING):

Calories: 298 | Fat: 17.1g | Cholesterol: 97mg | Total Carbohydrates: 6.4g | Sugar: 4.1g | Protein: 27g | Sodium: 185mg | Fiber: 2g

Refrigeration:
Store in an air-sealed container for up to 3 days.

Reheating:
Microwave for 1 minute or warm in the oven at 325°F.

INSTRUCTIONS

1. Preheat oven to 375°F (190°C). Arrange the baking tray with parchment paper.
2. Massage the ground turkey with salt and pepper.
3. Heat a skillet on moderate heat and cook turkey for 6–8 minutes, breaking it apart until browned.
4. Place bell pepper halves on the tray and fill with the cooked turkey.
5. Top with shredded cheese and bake for 10–12 minutes.
6. Let it sit for 2 minutes before serving.

SPINACH CHICKEN BOWL WITH FETA

PREP TIME
05 MINS

COOK TIME
10 MINS

SERVINGS
1

INGREDIENTS

- 1 boneless, skinless chicken breast (5 oz)
- 1 cup fresh spinach (for variety, use arugula or kale)
- 2 tbsp crumbled feta cheese (for dairy-free, use lactose-free feta)
- 1 tbsp olive oil (can be replaced with avocado oil)
- Salt & black pepper (to taste)

INSTRUCTIONS

1. Warm a skillet on moderate heat and drizzle with olive oil.
2. Massage the chicken breast with salt and pepper, then grill it for 5–6 minutes on one side until fully cooked.
3. Let the chicken sit for 3 minutes, then slice it.
4. Toss in spinach in the same skillet for 1 minute until wilted.
5. Plate the spinach and top with chicken slices and crumbled feta.

NUTRITIONAL VALUES (PER SERVING):

Calories: 313 | Fat: 14.1g | Cholesterol: 102mg | Total Carbohydrates: 2.1g | Sugar: 0.6g | Protein: 38.8g | Sodium: 298mg | Fiber: 0.7g

Refrigeration:
Store for up to 2 days.

Reheating:
Microwave chicken separately or warm in skillet for 2 minutes.

BROCCOLI & BACON SALAD

PREP TIME
05 MINS

COOK TIME
06 MINS

SERVINGS
1

INGREDIENTS

- 2 slices bacon
- 1 cup raw broccoli, chopped
- 1 tbsp mayonnaise (for egg-free, use avocado-based mayo)
- Salt & black pepper (to taste)
- 2 boiled eggs, sliced

INSTRUCTIONS

1. Cook bacon in a skillet on moderate heat until crisp, about 5–6 minutes. Let it sit, then chop finely.
2. Grab the shallow bowl and toss in the chopped broccoli, mayonnaise, salt, and pepper. Mix well.
3. Sprinkle the crispy bacon on top and toss again gently.
4. Serve chilled or at room temp.

NUTRITIONAL VALUES (PER SERVING):

Calories: 305 | Fat: 17.3g | Cholesterol: 26mg | Total Carbohydrates: 6.1g | Sugar: 1.5g | Protein: 29g | Sodium: 478mg | Fiber: 2.4g

Refrigeration:
Store covered for up to 2 days.

Reheating:
Not required.

AVOCADO CHICKEN SALAD

PREP TIME
05 MINS

COOK TIME
08 MINS

SERVINGS
1

NUTRITIONAL VALUES (PER SERVING):

Calories: 401 | Fat: 25g | Cholesterol: 101mg | Total Carbohydrates: 6.1g | Sugar: 0.2g | Protein: 36.6g | Sodium: 163mg | Fiber: 5g

Refrigeration:
Store in an air-sealed container for up to 1 day.

Reheating:
Not recommended; serve cold.

INGREDIENTS

- 1 boneless, skinless chicken breast (5 oz)
- ½ medium avocado, mashed
- 1 tbsp mayonnaise (for egg-free, use olive oil mayo)
- Salt & black pepper (to taste)

INSTRUCTIONS

1. Massage chicken with salt and pepper, then grill in a skillet with a little oil for 4–5 minutes on each side until cooked through.
2. Let it sit for 3 minutes, then shred or chop the chicken.
3. Grab the shallow bowl, mash the avocado, and mix it with mayonnaise.
4. Toss in the chicken and stir until everything is well coated.
5. Serve immediately or chill for later.

CRISPY TOFU & CABBAGE SLAW

PREP TIME

05 MINS

COOK TIME

10 MINS

SERVINGS

1

INGREDIENTS

- 4 oz firm tofu, cubed
- 1 cup cabbage, finely shredded
- 1 tbsp mayonnaise (for egg-free, use soy-free avocado mayo)
- 1 tbsp olive oil (or sesame oil for flavor)
- Salt & black pepper (to taste)

NUTRITIONAL VALUES (PER SERVING):

Calories: 292 | Fat: 24.1g | Cholesterol: 6mg | Total Carbohydrates: 6.2g | Sugar: 2.5g | Protein: 20.1g | Sodium: 116mg | Fiber: 2.7g

Refrigeration:
Store tofu and slaw separately for up to 2 days.

Reheating:
Re-crisp tofu in skillet for 2–3 minutes.

INSTRUCTIONS

1. Warm olive oil in a skillet and toss in cubed tofu. Sauté for 7–8 minutes until golden and crispy on all sides.
2. Grab the shallow bowl and toss cabbage with mayonnaise, salt, and crushed black pepper until well combined.
3. Top the slaw with hot, crispy tofu and serve immediately.

SMOKED SALMON & EGG SALAD

PREP TIME

05 MINS

COOK TIME

10 MINS

SERVINGS

1

INGREDIENTS

- 3 oz smoked salmon (choose wild-caught for cleaner flavor)
- 1 large egg
- 1 tbsp olive oil (can be replaced with avocado oil)
- Salt & black pepper (to taste)

INSTRUCTIONS

1. Boil the egg for 9–10 minutes, cool in ice water, then peel and chop.
2. Grab the shallow bowl and toss in chopped egg and flaked smoked salmon.
3. Drizzle with olive oil and gently mix.
4. Massage with salt and pepper and serve chilled or at room temp.

NUTRITIONAL VALUES (PER SERVING):

Calories: 321 | Fat: 24g | Cholesterol: 216mg | Total Carbohydrates: 0.6g | Sugar: 0.6g | Protein: 24g | Sodium: 730mg | Fiber: 0g

Refrigeration:
Store in an air-sealed container for up to 1 day.

Reheating:
Not recommended.

TUNA EGG STUFFED TOMATOES

PREP TIME

07 MINS

COOK TIME

10 MINS

SERVINGS

1

INGREDIENTS

- 1 large egg
- 3 oz canned tuna (in water)
- 1 medium tomato (can use Roma or heirloom)
- 1 tbsp mayonnaise (for egg-free, use olive oil mayo)

NUTRITIONAL VALUES (PER SERVING):

Calories: 285 | Fat: 16.2g | Cholesterol: 227mg | Total Carbohydrates: 5.5g | Sugar: 3.8g | Protein: 29.2g | Sodium: 374mg | Fiber: 1.5g

Refrigeration:
Best within 1 day. Store the tomato and filling separately if you are prepping ahead.

Reheating:
Not required.

INSTRUCTIONS

1. Boil the egg for 10 minutes, then chill, peel, and mash in a bowl.
2. Drain and flake the tuna, then mix with mashed egg and mayo.
3. Slice off the top of the tomato and scoop out the center.
4. Stuff the hollow tomato with the tuna-egg mixture.
5. Serve fresh, garnished with pepper if desired.

CAULIFLOWER TABBOULEH WITH CHICKEN

PREP TIME

06 MINS

COOK TIME

10 MINS

SERVINGS

1

INGREDIENTS

- 1 boneless chicken breast (3 oz)
- 1 cup cauliflower florets, finely chopped (for convenience, use riced cauliflower)
- ½ cup cucumber, diced
- 1 tbsp olive oil (can sub with lemon-infused oil)
- Salt & black pepper (to taste)

NUTRITIONAL VALUES (PER SERVING):

Calories: 294 | Fat: 17.4g | Cholesterol: 70mg | Total Carbohydrates: 7.2g | Sugar: 2.9g | Protein: 28.4g | Sodium: 93mg | Fiber: 2.4g

Refrigeration:
Store for up to 2 days.

Reheating:
Gently warm chicken before mixing if desired.

INSTRUCTIONS

1. Massage chicken with salt and pepper. Grill on skillet for 4–5 minutes on one side until cooked through. Let it sit and slice.
2. Steam or lightly sauté cauliflower for 2 minutes, just until tender.
3. Toss in the cucumber and olive oil.
4. Combine with chicken slices and mix gently.
5. Serve warm or chilled.

TUNA NORI SEAWEED WRAPS

PREP TIME

05 MINS

COOK TIME

00 MINS

SERVINGS

1

NUTRITIONAL VALUES (PER SERVING):

Calories: 211 | Fat: 11.2g | Cholesterol: 41mg | Total Carbohydrates: 3g | Sugar: 0.9g | Protein: 23.4g | Sodium: 314mg | Fiber: 0.6g

Refrigeration:
Best eaten fresh. It can be refrigerated for 4–6 hours and wrapped.

Reheating:
Not applicable.

INGREDIENTS

- 3 oz canned tuna (in water)
- 1 sheet nori (seaweed)
- 1 tbsp mayonnaise (for egg-free, use avocado mayo)
- ½ cup cucumber, sliced into matchsticks
- Salt & black pepper (to taste)

INSTRUCTIONS

1. Grab the shallow bowl and mash tuna with mayo, salt, and pepper.
2. Lay the nori sheet flat on a clean surface.
3. Spread tuna mixture across the center and top with cucumber slices.
4. Roll it tightly and let it sit for 2 minutes to set.
5. Slice in half and serve fresh.

CHILI LIME SHRIMP & CAULIFLOWER RICE BOWL

PREP TIME

05 MINS

COOK TIME

10 MINS

SERVINGS

1

INGREDIENTS

- 4 oz raw shrimp, peeled and deveined
- 1 cup cauliflower florets, grated or riced
- 1 tbsp lime juice
- 1 tbsp olive oil (can sub with chili-infused oil)
- Salt, pepper, chili flakes (to taste)

NUTRITIONAL VALUES (PER SERVING):

Calories: 270 | Fat: 15.8g | Cholesterol: 170mg | Total Carbohydrates: 7.6g | Sugar: 2.3g | Protein: 25.2g | Sodium: 213mg | Fiber: 2.1g

Refrigeration:
Store for up to 1 day.

Reheating:
Lightly warm in skillet for best texture.

INSTRUCTIONS

1. Heat one tbsp oil in a skillet. Toss in shrimp, salt, crushed pepper, and chili flakes. Cook for 2–3 minutes on one side until pink.
2. Remove shrimp and toss in riced cauliflower. Cook for 2–3 minutes until tender.
3. Return shrimp to the pan and ladle lime juice over the bowl.
4. Let it sit for 2 minutes, then serve warm.

DINNER

ENTREES

LEMON GARLIC BUTTER CHICKEN

PREP TIME

05 MINS

COOK TIME

12 MINS

SERVINGS

1

NUTRITIONAL VALUES (PER SERVING):

Calories: 387 | Fat: 17.5g | Cholesterol: 175mg | Total Carbohydrates: 2g | Sugar: 0.1g | Protein: 52.5g | Sodium: 102mg | Fiber: 0.1g

Refrigeration:
Store in an air-sealed container for up to 2 days.

Reheating:
Warm in skillet for 2–3 minutes or microwave for 1 minute.

INGREDIENTS

- 1 boneless, skinless chicken breast (6 oz)
- 1 tbsp butter (for dairy-free, use ghee or olive oil)
- 2 garlic cloves, minced
- Salt, black pepper, lemon zest (to taste)

INSTRUCTIONS

1. Massage the chicken breast with salt, crushed pepper, and lemon zest.
2. Melt butter in a skillet on moderate heat and toss in minced garlic. Sauté 30 seconds.
3. Place the chicken breast in the pan and sear for 5–6 minutes on one side until golden and cooked thoroughly.
4. Spoon the lemon-garlic butter over the chicken before serving.

HERB-CRUSTED SALMON

PREP TIME

05 MINS

COOK TIME

10 MINS

SERVINGS

1

INGREDIENTS

- 6 oz salmon fillet
- 1 tbsp butter (for dairy-free, use olive oil)
- 2 garlic cloves, minced
- 1 tbsp mixed dried herbs (parsley, dill, oregano)
- Salt & black pepper (to taste)

NUTRITIONAL VALUES (PER SERVING):

Calories: 478 | Fat: 33.5g | Cholesterol: 125mg | Total Carbohydrates: 2g | Sugar: 0.1g | Protein: 39.5g | Sodium: 102mg | Fiber: 0.1g

Refrigeration:
Store in a container for up to 2 days.

Reheating:
Reheat gently in a pan or oven at 300°F.

INSTRUCTIONS

1. Massage salmon with salt, crushed pepper, and herbs. Melt butter in a skillet and toss in mashed garlic.
2. Place the salmon skin-side down and cook for 4–5 minutes. Flip and cook more for 3–4 minutes until done.
3. Let it sit for 1 minute before plating.

GARLIC HERB LAMB CHOPS

PREP TIME

05 MINS

COOK TIME

10 MINS

SERVINGS

1

INGREDIENTS

- 2 lamb chops (about 5–6 oz total)
- 1 tbsp olive oil (or avocado oil)
- 1 garlic clove, minced
- 1 tsp fresh rosemary or thyme (or ½ tsp dried)
- Salt & black pepper (to taste

NUTRITIONAL VALUES (PER SERVING):

Calories: 354 | Fat: 27.4g | Cholesterol: 87mg | Total Carbohydrates: 0.6g | Sugar: 0g | Protein: 27.6g | Sodium: 85mg | Fiber: 0g

Refrigeration:
Store in a container for up to 2 days.

Reheating:
Rewarm in a skillet over low heat or microwave for 1–2 minutes.

INSTRUCTIONS

1. Pat lamb chops dry and massage with olive oil, garlic, rosemary, salt, and pepper. Let sit for a couple of minutes while the skillet heats.
2. Heat a skillet on moderate heat. Once hot, add the lamb chops and sear for about 3–4 minutes per side for medium-rare, adjusting time for your desired doneness.
3. Spoon pan juices over the lamb during the final minute of cooking, then let rest for 2 minutes before serving.

STUFFED CHICKEN BREAST WITH CREAM CHEESE

PREP TIME
06 MINS

COOK TIME
14 MINS

SERVINGS
1

NUTRITIONAL VALUES (PER SERVING):

Calories: 385 | Fat: 16g | Cholesterol: 174mg | Total Carbohydrates: 3g | Sugar: 1.1g | Protein: 54.4g | Sodium: 191mg | Fiber: 0.1g

Refrigeration:
Keep in an air-sealed container for 2 days.

Reheating:
Warm in the oven at 325°F for 5–7 minutes.

INGREDIENTS

- 6 oz chicken breast
- 2 tbsp cream cheese (for dairy-free, use almond or cashew cream cheese)
- 2 garlic cloves, minced
- Salt & pepper (to taste)

INSTRUCTIONS

1. Slice a pocket in the side of the chicken breast.
2. Grab the shallow bowl and mix cream cheese with garlic and salt (just a pinch).
3. Stuff the mixture into the meat and secure with toothpicks if needed.
4. Sear the stuffed chicken in a skillet for 6 minutes on one side, then let it sit for 2 minutes.

KETO BEEF STIR-FRY

PREP TIME
05 MINS

COOK TIME
12 MINS

SERVINGS
1

INGREDIENTS

- 6 oz ground beef (85% lean)
- ½ cup chopped broccoli
- ½ cup sliced bell pepper
- 2 garlic cloves, minced
- Salt, pepper, chili flakes (to taste)

NUTRITIONAL VALUES (PER SERVING):

Calories: 465 | Fat: 34.3g | Cholesterol: 114mg | Total Carbohydrates: 8.5g | Sugar: 3.1g | Protein: 29.2g | Sodium: 92mg | Fiber: 2g

Refrigeration:
Store for up to 2 days.

Reheating:
Pan-fry again for 2–3 minutes or microwave for 1 minute.

INSTRUCTIONS

1. Heat a skillet on moderate heat and toss in ground beef with garlic and seasonings.
2. Cook beef for 6–7 minutes until browned.
3. Add broccoli florets and bell peppers and cook for 4–5 minutes until tender.
4. Let it sit for 2 minutes before serving.

BAKED COD WITH LEMON & OLIVE OIL

PREP TIME

05 MINS

COOK TIME

12 MINS

SERVINGS

1

INGREDIENTS

- 6 oz raw cod fillet
- 1 tbsp olive oil (for stronger flavor, use garlic-infused olive oil)
- 2 garlic cloves, minced
- Salt, pepper, lemon juice & zest (to taste)

NUTRITIONAL VALUES (PER SERVING):

Calories: 266 | Fat: 15.3g | Cholesterol: 63mg | Total Carbohydrates: 2g | Sugar: 0.1g | Protein: 30.4g | Sodium: 106mg | Fiber: 0.1g

Refrigeration:
Store in an air-sealed container for up to 2 days.

Reheating:
Gently re-heat in the oven at 300°F for 5 minutes.

INSTRUCTIONS

1. Preheat oven to 375°F (190°C). Arrange the baking sheet with parchment paper.
2. Massage cod with one tbsp oil, salt, crushed pepper, and lemon zest.
3. Top with minced garlic and bake for 12 minutes or until fish flakes easily.
4. Drizzle lemon juice (one tbsp) and let it sit for 1 minute before serving.

KETO PORK CHOPS WITH HERBS

PREP TIME
05 MINS

COOK TIME
15 MINS

SERVINGS
1

INGREDIENTS

- 6 oz pork chop
- 1 tbsp butter (for dairy-free, use olive oil)
- 2 garlic cloves, minced
- 1 tsp dried herbs (rosemary, thyme, or oregano)
- Salt & black pepper (to taste)

INSTRUCTIONS

1. Massage pork chop with salt, crushed pepper, and dried herbs.
2. Melt butter in a skillet on moderate heat and toss in the garlic.
3. Sear pork chop for 6–7 minutes on each side until golden and cooked through.
4. Put it aside to cool for 2–3 minutes before slicing and serving.

NUTRITIONAL VALUES (PER SERVING):

Calories: 446 | Fat: 33.5g | Cholesterol: 119mg | Total Carbohydrates: 2g | Sugar: 0.1g | Protein: 32.5g | Sodium: 82mg | Fiber: 0.1g

Refrigeration:
Store for up to 2 days in an air-sealed container.

Reheating:
Warm in skillet for 3 minutes or microwave for 1 minute.

SHRIMP SKEWERS WITH GARLIC MARINADE

PREP TIME

10 MINS

COOK TIME

06 MINS

SERVINGS

1

INGREDIENTS

- 6 oz raw shrimp, peeled and deveined
- 1 tbsp olive oil (or use avocado oil)
- 2 garlic cloves, minced
- Salt, chili flakes, lemon zest (to taste)

NUTRITIONAL VALUES (PER SERVING):

Calories: 308 | Fat: 16.3g | Cholesterol: 255mg | Total Carbohydrates: 3.5g | Sugar: 0.1g | Protein: 35.4g | Sodium: 271mg | Fiber: 0.1g

Refrigeration:
Store for up to 1 day.

Reheating:
Re-grill for 2 minutes or microwave briefly.

INSTRUCTIONS

1. Grab the shallow bowl and mix shrimp with oil, garlic, salt, and chili flakes. Let it sit for 5 minutes.
2. Thread shrimp onto skewers.
3. Heat grill pan and cook for 2–3 minutes on one side until pink and firm.
4. Put it aside to rest for 1 minute before serving with lemon zest.

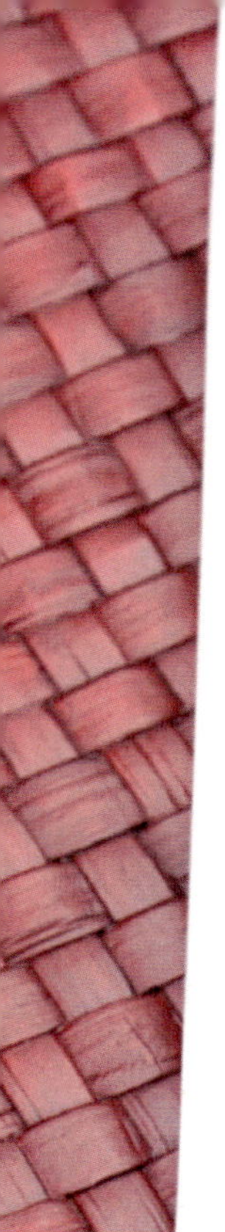

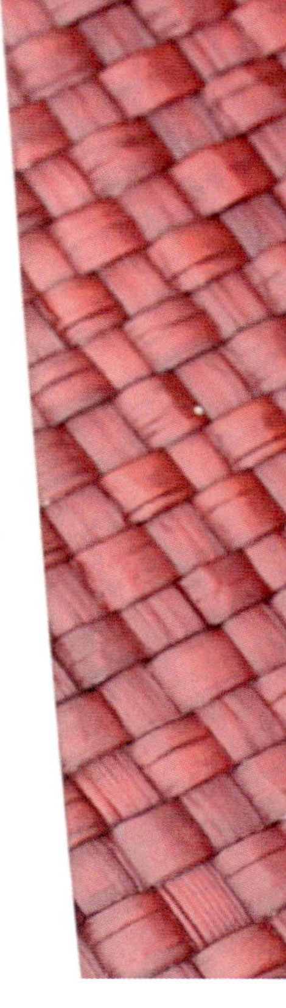

KETO LAMB BURGERS

PREP TIME
05 MINS

COOK TIME
10 MINS

SERVINGS
1

NUTRITIONAL VALUES (PER SERVING):

Calories: 598 | Fat: 52g | Cholesterol: 105mg | Total Carbohydrates: 2g | Sugar: 0.1g | Protein: 30.4g | Sodium: 76mg | Fiber: 0.1g

Refrigeration:
Store for 2 days in an air-sealed container.

Reheating:
Reheat in skillet or oven for best texture.

INGREDIENTS

- 6 oz ground lamb
- 2 garlic cloves, minced
- 1 tbsp ghee (can be replaced with olive oil for dairy-free)
- Salt, pepper, herbs (to taste)

INSTRUCTIONS

1. Grab the shallow bowl and mix lamb with garlic, salt, crushed pepper, and herbs. Shape
2. into a thick patty.
3. Heat one tbsp oil in a skillet on moderate heat.
4. Cook patty for 4–5 minutes on each side until browned and done to your liking.
5. Let it sit 2 minutes before serving.

ZUCCHINI LASAGNA WITH GROUND TURKEY

PREP TIME

07 MINS

COOK TIME

15 MINS

SERVINGS

1

NUTRITIONAL VALUES (PER SERVING):

Calories: 295 | Fat: 15.8g | Cholesterol: 100mg | Total Carbohydrates: 8.9g | Sugar: 5.5g | Protein: 30.5g | Sodium: 390mg | Fiber: 2.2g

Refrigeration:
Store for up to 2 days in a container.

Reheating:
Warm in oven or microwave.

INGREDIENTS

- 4 oz ground turkey
- 1 cup zucchini, thinly sliced
- ¼ cup no-sugar tomato sauce
- ¼ cup shredded mozzarella cheese (for dairy-free, use almond mozzarella)
- Salt & black pepper (to taste)

INSTRUCTIONS

1. Heat a skillet and cook turkey with salt and pepper for 6–7 minutes until browned.
2. In a baking dish, layer zucchini, tomato sauce, ground turkey, and cheese.
3. Repeat layers and top with cheese.
4. Bake at 375°F (190°C) for 10 minutes until bubbly.
5. Let it sit for 3 minutes before serving.

BAKED CHICKEN DRUMSTICKS WITH PAPRIKA

PREP TIME
05 MINS

COOK TIME
30 MINS

SERVINGS
1

INGREDIENTS

- 2 medium chicken drumsticks (~6 oz total)
- 1 tbsp olive oil (or you can use avocado oil)
- 2 garlic cloves, minced
- 1 tsp paprika
- Salt & black pepper (to taste)

NUTRITIONAL VALUES (PER SERVING):

Calories: 382 | Fat: 29.3g | Cholesterol: 120mg | Total Carbohydrates: 2g | Sugar: 0.1g | Protein: 28.4g | Sodium: 101mg | Fiber: 0.1g

Refrigeration:
Store in an air-sealed container for up to 3 days.

Reheating:
Oven at 325°F for 10 minutes or microwave for 1–2 minutes.

INSTRUCTIONS

1. Preheat oven to 400°F (200°C). Arrange the baking tray with foil or parchment.
2. Massage drumsticks with oil, paprika, garlic, salt, and pepper.
3. Place on a tray and bake for 25–30 minutes, flipping halfway.
4. Let it sit for 2 minutes before serving hot.

KETO CHICKEN ALFREDO

PREP TIME

05 MINS

COOK TIME

12 MINS

SERVINGS

1

INGREDIENTS

- 1 boneless, skinless chicken breast (6 oz)
- 2 tbsp heavy cream (for lactose-sensitive, use coconut cream)
- 2 tbsp grated Parmesan cheese (for dairy-free, use nutritional yeast)
- 2 garlic cloves, minced
- Salt & black pepper (to taste)

INSTRUCTIONS

1. Slice chicken into strips and massage with salt and pepper.
2. In a skillet, cook chicken for 5–6 minutes on one side until browned and cooked through. Remove and set aside.
3. In the same skillet, toss in garlic and sauté for 30 seconds.
4. Stir in cream and Parmesan, cooking for 2–3 minutes to thicken.
5. Return the meat to the pan and toss to coat. Serve warm.

NUTRITIONAL VALUES (PER SERVING):

Calories: 427 | Fat: 18.8g | Cholesterol: 191mg | Total Carbohydrates: 3.3g | Sugar: 1.1g | Protein: 56.7g | Sodium: 187mg | Fiber: 0.1g

Refrigeration:
Store for up to 2 days.

Reheating:
Warm in a skillet on low heat or microwave for 1 minute.

STEAK WITH MUSHROOM SAUCE

PREP TIME

05 MINS

COOK TIME

10 MINS

SERVINGS

1

NUTRITIONAL VALUES (PER SERVING):

Calories: 443 | Fat: 29.6g | Cholesterol: 131mg | Total Carbohydrates: 3.5g | Sugar: 0.6g | Protein: 39.5g | Sodium: 69mg | Fiber: 0.6g

Refrigeration:
Store for up to 2 days.

Reheating:
Reheat in a skillet with a splash of broth or butter.

INGREDIENTS

- 5 oz sirloin steak
- ½ cup mushrooms, chopped
- 1 tbsp butter (for dairy-free, use ghee or olive oil)
- 2 garlic cloves, minced
- Salt & pepper (to taste)

INSTRUCTIONS

1. Massage steak with salt and pepper.
2. Heat butter in a skillet, sear steak for 4–5 minutes on one side. Let it sit after cooking.
3. In the same pan, toss in garlic and mushrooms. Sauté 3–4 minutes until browned.
4. Plate steak and top with the mushroom sauce.

SPICY GRILLED SHRIMP WITH HERBS

PREP TIME

05 MINS

COOK TIME

06 MINS

SERVINGS

1

NUTRITIONAL VALUES (PER SERVING):

Calories: 308 | Fat: 16.3g | Cholesterol: 255mg | Total Carbohydrates: 3.5g | Sugar: 0.1g | Protein: 35.4g | Sodium: 271mg | Fiber: 0.1g

Refrigeration:
Store for up to 1 day.

Reheating:
Briefly reheat in skillet or microwave.

INGREDIENTS

- 6 oz raw shrimp, peeled and deveined
- 1 tbsp olive oil (or use chili-infused oil)
- 2 garlic cloves, minced
- 1 tsp mixed herbs (thyme, oregano)
- Salt, chili flakes, black pepper (to taste)

INSTRUCTIONS

1. In a shallow dish, mix the shrimp with olive oil, garlic, herbs, and spices until well coated. Let it marinate for 5 minutes.
2. Heat a grill pan on moderate heat. Arrange the shrimp in a single layer.
3. Cook for 2–3 minutes on one side, until pink and fully cooked through.
4. Serve immediately while hot and flavorful.

TURKEY PATTIES WITH CREAMY SPINACH

PREP TIME

06 MINS

COOK TIME

12 MINS

SERVINGS

1

INGREDIENTS

- 5 oz ground turkey
- 1 cup spinach, chopped
- 2 tbsp cream cheese (for dairy-free, use cashew cream)
- 2 garlic cloves, minced
- Salt & black pepper (to taste)

NUTRITIONAL VALUES (PER SERVING):

Calories: 362 | Fat: 20.5g | Cholesterol: 120mg | Total Carbohydrates: 10g | Sugar: 1.5g | Protein: 34.8g | Sodium: 302mg | Fiber: 4.4g

Refrigeration:
Store for up to 2 days.

Reheating:
Microwave for 1 minute or reheat in a skillet.

INSTRUCTIONS

1. Form the turkey into 2 small patties. Season with salt and pepper.
2. In a skillet, cook patties for 4–5 minutes on one side until fully cooked. Remove and set aside.
3. In the same skillet, toss in garlic and spinach. Cook 1–2 minutes.
4. Stir in cream cheese and cook until creamy.
5. Plate turkey patties over spinach and serve.

SOUPS & STEWS

CREAMY CHICKEN & MUSHROOM SOUP

PREP TIME
05 MINS

COOK TIME
15 MINS

SERVINGS
1

INGREDIENTS

- 4 oz boneless chicken breast
- ½ cup chopped mushrooms
- ¼ cup heavy cream (for lactose-free, use full-fat coconut cream)
- 2 garlic cloves, minced
- Salt & black pepper (to taste)

NUTRITIONAL VALUES (PER SERVING):

Calories: 403 | Fat: 26.1g | Cholesterol: 176mg | Total Carbohydrates: 5.5g | Sugar: 2.6g | Protein: 37.4g | Sodium: 93mg | Fiber: 0.6g

Refrigeration:
Store for up to 2 days.

Reheating:
Simmer on the stovetop or microwave for 1–2 minutes.

INSTRUCTIONS

1. Dice chicken into small cubes and massage with salt and pepper.
2. In a pot, heat one tbsp oil and sauté mashed garlic and mushrooms for 2–3 minutes.
3. Add boneless chicken and cook for 5–6 minutes until golden.
4. Ladle in heavy cream and simmer for 4–5 minutes, stirring gently.
5. Let it sit for 2 minutes before serving hot.

KETO BROCCOLI CHEDDAR SOUP

PREP TIME	COOK TIME	SERVINGS
05 MINS	10 MINS	1

INGREDIENTS

- 1 cup chopped broccoli
- ¼ cup shredded cheddar cheese (use lactose-free cheddar if needed)
- ¼ cup heavy cream (can sub with coconut cream)
- 2 garlic cloves, minced
- Salt & black pepper (to taste)

INSTRUCTIONS

1. Sauté mashed garlic in a pot with a splash of oil for 30 seconds.
2. Add broccoli and ½ cup water, simmer for 5 minutes until soft.
3. Stir in cream and cheese, then simmer 2 more minutes until melted.
4. Blend for a smooth texture, or leave it chunky. Serve hot.

NUTRITIONAL VALUES (PER SERVING):

Calories: 350 | Fat: 31.4g | Cholesterol: 110mg | Total Carbohydrates: 11g | Sugar: 3.6g | Protein: 10.9g | Sodium: 231mg | Fiber: 2.5g

Refrigeration:
Store for up to 2 days.

Reheating:
Microwave 1 minute or simmer gently.

CHICKEN ZUCCHINI BASIL SOUP

PREP TIME
05 MINS

COOK TIME
12 MINS

SERVINGS
1

INGREDIENTS

- 1 cup chopped zucchini
- 1 tbsp olive oil (can use avocado oil)
- ½ cup cooked and shredded chicken breast (prepare fresh within the recipe)
- ½ cup water
- Salt & black pepper (to taste)

NUTRITIONAL VALUES (PER SERVING):

Calories: 234 | Fat: 14.3g | Cholesterol: 59mg | Total Carbohydrates: 6.3g | Sugar: 2.8g | Protein: 23.2g | Sodium: 112mg | Fiber: 1.4g

Refrigeration:
Store in an air-sealed container for up to 2 days.

Reheating:
Warm gently on the stovetop or in the microwave before serving.

INSTRUCTIONS

1. Heat one tbsp oil in a saucepan on moderate heat. Add zucchini and cook for 4–5 minutes, stirring occasionally, until softened.
2. Toss in the shredded chicken and stir well to heat through evenly.
3. Add fresh basil and ½ cup water. Let it simmer for 2–3 minutes, let the flavors to get infuse.
4. Blend briefly if desired, or serve as a hearty, chunky soup with tender chicken in every bite.

BEEF & SPINACH STEW

PREP TIME
05 MINS

COOK TIME
15 MINS

SERVINGS
1

INGREDIENTS

- 5 oz ground beef (85% lean)
- 1 cup fresh spinach
- 2 garlic cloves, minced
- 1 tbsp olive oil (or use beef tallow)
- Salt, pepper, paprika (to taste)

NUTRITIONAL VALUES (PER SERVING):

Calories: 490 | Fat: 42.1g | Cholesterol: 95mg | Total Carbohydrates: 3.1g | Sugar: 0.2g | Protein: 24.3g | Sodium: 90mg | Fiber: 0.8g

Refrigeration:
Store for up to 2 days.

Reheating:
Reheat the stove for the best taste.

INSTRUCTIONS

1. Heat one tbsp oil in a pot and sauté mashed garlic for 1 minute.
2. Add minced beef and cook for 6–7 minutes until browned.
3. Toss in spinach and stir until wilted.
4. Add ¼ cup water and simmer for 3–4 minutes for flavor to meld.
5. Serve warm.

SHRIMP & COCONUT MILK SOUP

PREP TIME
05 MINS

COOK TIME
10 MINS

SERVINGS
1

INGREDIENTS

- 5 oz raw shrimp, peeled and deveined
- ¼ cup full-fat coconut milk (no substitute needed)
- 2 garlic cloves, minced
- 1 tbsp olive oil (or use coconut oil)
- Salt, chili flakes, ginger (to taste)

NUTRITIONAL VALUES (PER SERVING):

Calories: 378 | Fat: 25.5g | Cholesterol: 215mg | Total Carbohydrates: 5.2g | Sugar: 1.1g | Protein: 30.4g | Sodium: 226mg | Fiber: 0.1g

Refrigeration:
Store for up to 1 day.

Reheating:
Reheat in pot gently to avoid overcooking shrimp.

INSTRUCTIONS

1. Heat one tbsp oil in a saucepan, add mashed garlic and grated ginger, and sauté for 1 minute.
2. Add shrimp and cook for 3 minutes until pink.
3. Ladle in coconut milk and simmer for 3–4 minutes.
4. Season with chili flakes and salt. Let it sit 1 minute before serving.

TURKEY & CAULIFLOWER RICE SOUP

PREP TIME

05 MINS

COOK TIME

15 MINS

SERVINGS

1

INGREDIENTS

- 4 oz ground turkey
- 1 cup cauliflower rice (or freshly grated cauliflower)
- 2 garlic cloves, minced
- 1 tbsp olive oil (substitute: avocado oil)
- Salt, pepper, chili flakes (to taste)

NUTRITIONAL VALUES (PER SERVING):

Calories: 323 | Fat: 22.1g | Cholesterol: 75mg | Total Carbohydrates: 7g | Sugar: 2.1g | Protein: 24.4g | Sodium: 101mg | Fiber: 2.1g

Refrigeration:
Store in an air-sealed container for up to 2 days.

Reheating:
Microwave for 1–2 minutes or reheat on stovetop.

INSTRUCTIONS

1. Heat one tbsp oil in a pot and sauté mashed garlic until fragrant.
2. Add ground turkey and break it apart while cooking for 5–6 minutes until no pink remains.
3. Toss in cauliflower rice and stir everything together.
4. Add ½ cup water and simmer covered for 3–4 minutes.
5. Remove the lid and cook more for 1–2 minutes to thicken slightly.
6. Ladle into the deep-bottom bowl, garnish with chili flakes and enjoy hot.

TOFU & BOK CHOY MISO SOUP

PREP TIME

05 MINS

COOK TIME

10 MINS

SERVINGS

1

INGREDIENTS

- 4 oz firm tofu, cubed
- 1 cup bok choy, chopped
- 1 tbsp miso paste (use low-sodium miso if needed)
- 2 garlic cloves, minced
- Salt & sesame seeds (optional)

NUTRITIONAL VALUES (PER SERVING):

Calories: 147 | Fat: 7g | Cholesterol: 0mg | Total Carbohydrates: 9.8g | Sugar: 2.4g | Protein: 13.5g | Sodium: 690mg | Fiber: 1.8g

Refrigeration:
Store for up to 1 day.

Reheating:
Gently warm over low heat.

INSTRUCTIONS

1. Heat one cup water in a saucepan and whisk in miso paste until dissolved.
2. Add tofu cubes and simmer for 3–4 minutes to absorb flavor.
3. Toss in bok choy and garlic, and cook another 4 minutes until wilted.
4. Add a pinch of salt if needed and stir gently.
5. Let it sit off heat for 2 minutes to meld flavors.
6. Serve warm with sesame seeds or chopped scallions if desired.

SPICY SAUSAGE & KALE SOUP

PREP TIME
05 MINS

COOK TIME
15 MINS

SERVINGS
1

INGREDIENTS

- 4 oz raw pork sausage, crumbled
- 1 cup chopped kale
- 2 garlic cloves, minced
- 1 tbsp olive oil (or use sausage drippings)
- Chili flakes, pepper (to taste)

NUTRITIONAL VALUES (PER SERVING):

Calories: 491 | Fat: 42.6g | Cholesterol: 65mg | Total Carbohydrates: 10g | Sugar: 1.4g | Protein: 17.3g | Sodium: 750mg | Fiber: 1.4g

Refrigeration:
Store for up to 2 days.

Reheating:
Simmer for 3–4 minutes or microwave briefly.

INSTRUCTIONS

1. Heat skillet and brown sausage for 5–6 minutes, breaking apart.
2. Transfer sausage to a soup pot and add garlic and oil.
3. Toss in kale and sauté until it wilts.
4. Add ½ cup water and simmer on low for 5–6 minutes.
5. Sprinkle chili flakes and pepper, and stir well.
6. Let it rest for 2 minutes before serving hot and spicy.

EGG DROP SPINACH SOUP

PREP TIME
03 MINS

COOK TIME
05 MINS

SERVINGS
1

NUTRITIONAL VALUES (PER SERVING):

Calories: 204 | Fat: 18.9g | Cholesterol: 186mg | Total Carbohydrates: 3.2g | Sugar: 0.8g | Protein: 7.2g | Sodium: 86mg | Fiber: 0.5g

Refrigeration:
Best consumed immediately.

Reheating:
Reheat gently on the stovetop.

INGREDIENTS

- 1 large egg
- ½ cup chopped spinach
- 2 garlic cloves, minced
- 1 tbsp olive oil
- Salt, ginger powder, black pepper (to taste)

INSTRUCTIONS

1. Heat one tbsp oil in a saucepan and sauté mashed garlic and spinach for 1 minute.
2. Add 1 cup water and get it it to a light boil.
3. Beat the egg in a small shallow bowl.
4. Slowly drizzle the egg into the simmering broth while stirring gently.
5. Cook more for 1–2 minutes until egg strands form.
6. Add salt, pepper, and ginger powder. Serve warm.

GARLIC CHICKEN BONE BROTH

PREP TIME
02 MINS

COOK TIME
05 MINS

SERVINGS
1

INGREDIENTS

- 1 cup chicken bone broth (low-sodium preferred)
- 2 garlic cloves, minced
- 1 tbsp olive oil (can sub with ghee)
- Salt, pepper, turmeric (optional)

NUTRITIONAL VALUES (PER SERVING):

Calories: 168 | Fat: 15.5g | Cholesterol: 5mg | Total Carbohydrates: 3g | Sugar: 0.1g | Protein: 7.4g | Sodium: 151mg | Fiber: 0.1g

Refrigeration:
Store for up to 2 days.

Reheating:
Microwave or simmer on low heat.

INSTRUCTIONS

1. In a saucepan, heat one tbsp oil and sauté mashed garlic for 1 minute until golden. Ladle in the chicken bone broth and get it to a simmer.
2. Add turmeric, salt, and crushed black pepper to taste. Let it simmer on low for 4 minutes to develop flavor.
3. Strain if desired for a smooth sip. Ladle into a mug and sip warm like a tonic.

CREAMY TOMATO BASIL SOUP

PREP TIME
05 MINS

COOK TIME
10 MINS

SERVINGS
1

INGREDIENTS

- ½ cup canned tomato
- 1 tbsp fresh basil, chopped
- ¼ cup heavy cream (use coconut cream for dairy-free)
- 2 garlic cloves, minced
- Salt & pepper (to taste)

NUTRITIONAL VALUES (PER SERVING):

Calories: 230 | Fat: 22.2g | Cholesterol: 80mg | Total Carbohydrates: 8.7g | Sugar: 5.6g | Protein: 2.5g | Sodium: 162mg | Fiber: 1.4g

Refrigeration:
Store for up to 2 days.

Reheating:
Microwave for 1 minute or simmer on low heat.

INSTRUCTIONS

1. Heat a saucepan and sauté mashed garlic for 1 minute until fragrant. Add canned tomato and cook for 4–5 minutes to reduce liquid.
2. Toss in basil and cook 1 more minute. Add cream, reduce heat, and stir well.
3. Simmer for 2–3 minutes until creamy.
4. Blend for a smoother texture, or serve chunky with a drizzle of olive oil.

CHICKEN ZOODLE SOUP

PREP TIME

05 MINS

COOK TIME

12 MINS

SERVINGS

1

INGREDIENTS

- 4 oz chicken breast, diced
- 1 cup zucchini noodles
- 2 garlic cloves, minced
- 1 tbsp olive oil (can sub with avocado oil)
- Salt, pepper, thyme (to taste)

NUTRITIONAL VALUES (PER SERVING):

Calories: 332 | Fat: 18.3g | Cholesterol: 96mg | Total Carbohydrates: 5.9g | Sugar: 2.8g | Protein: 36.9g | Sodium: 76mg | Fiber: 1.3g

Refrigeration:
Store for up to 2 days.

Reheating:
Warm in the microwave or on the stovetop until heated through.

INSTRUCTIONS

1. Heat one tbsp oil in a pot and sauté mashed garlic for 1 minute. Add chicken breast pieces and cook for 6–7 minutes until fully cooked.
2. Ladle in ½ cup water and get it to a gentle boil. Add zucchini noodles and simmer for 2–3 minutes.
3. Add thyme, salt, and pepper, then stir gently. Put it aside to sit for 1 minute before serving warm.

BEEF CABBAGE SOUP

PREP TIME

05 MINS

COOK TIME

12 MINS

SERVINGS

1

INGREDIENTS

- 4 oz ground beef (85% lean)
- 1 cup chopped cabbage
- 2 garlic cloves, minced
- 1 tbsp olive oil (or use beef drippings)
- Salt, black pepper, chili flakes (to taste)

NUTRITIONAL VALUES (PER SERVING):

Calories: 434 | Fat: 37.1g | Cholesterol: 76mg | Total Carbohydrates: 7.2g | Sugar: 2.9g | Protein: 20.7g | Sodium: 71mg | Fiber: 2.3g

Refrigeration:
Store in the fridge for up to 2 days.

Reheating:
Microwave for 1–2 minutes or simmer on the stove.

INSTRUCTIONS

1. Heat one tbsp oil in a deep pot and cook garlic for 30 seconds. Add ground beef and brown for 5–6 minutes.
2. Toss in chopped cabbage and stir together. Ladle in ½ cup water and get it to a light boil.
3. Cover and simmer for 3–4 minutes. Stir again and serve hot with chili flakes if desired.

MUSHROOM COCONUT CURRY SOUP

PREP TIME
05 MINS

COOK TIME
10 MINS

SERVINGS
1

INGREDIENTS

- ½ cup chopped mushrooms
- ¼ cup full-fat coconut milk
- 2 garlic cloves, minced
- 1 tbsp olive oil (can be swapped with coconut oil)
- Salt, curry powder, ginger (to taste)

NUTRITIONAL VALUES (PER SERVING):

Calories: 238 | Fat: 24.1g | Cholesterol: 0mg | Total Carbohydrates: 5.5g | Sugar: 1.6g | Protein: 2.4g | Sodium: 8mg | Fiber: 0.6g

Refrigeration:
Store up to 2 days.

Reheating:
Microwave gently or simmer for 2–3 minutes.

INSTRUCTIONS

1. Heat one tbsp oil in a pot and sauté mashed garlic for 30 seconds. Add mushrooms and cook 3–4 minutes until softened.
2. Ladle in coconut milk and ½ cup water. Add curry powder, salt, and ginger. Simmer uncovered for 4–5 minutes.
3. Serve warm with fresh herbs or chili flakes.

SALMON MISO BROTH

PREP TIME
05 MINS

COOK TIME
08 MINS

SERVINGS
1

NUTRITIONAL VALUES (PER SERVING):

Calories: 386 | Fat: 29g | Cholesterol: 62mg | Total Carbohydrates: 4.5g | Sugar: 1.1g | Protein: 26.7g | Sodium: 481mg | Fiber: 0.1g

Refrigeration:
Store in an airtight container for up to 2 days.

Reheating:

Gently reheat on the stovetop over low heat. Avoid boiling to preserve the delicate miso flavor and texture of the salmon.

INGREDIENTS

- 4 oz salmon, diced
- 2 tsp miso paste (low-sodium preferred)
- 2 garlic cloves, minced
- 1 tbsp olive oil (or use sesame oil)
- Optional: chopped scallions, chili oil

INSTRUCTIONS

1. Heat one tbsp oil in a small pot and add garlic. Cook for 1 minute. Add salmon cubes and sear for 2–3 minutes until golden on the edges.
2. Stir in 1 cup water and get it to a simmer.
3. Whisk in miso paste until dissolved. Cook more for 2 minutes on low heat. Garnish with scallions and serve hot.

SIDE DISHES

BACON-WRAPPED ASPARAGUS BUNDLES

PREP TIME
10 MINS

COOK TIME
15 MINS

SERVINGS
2

INGREDIENTS

- 12 asparagus spears
- 6 slices turkey bacon
- 1 tbsp olive oil
- Black pepper (to taste)

NUTRITIONAL VALUES (PER SERVING):

Calories: 170 | Fat: 12g | Cholesterol: 30mg | Carbs: 3g | Sugar: 1g | Protein: 13g | Sodium: 390mg

Refrigeration:
Store up to 2 days.

Reheating:
Reheat in oven at 350°F until warm.

INSTRUCTIONS

1. Preheat oven to 400°F (200°C). Wash and trim the woody ends off asparagus spears.
2. Wrap 2 spears with 1 slice of bacon and repeat for all.
3. Place bundles on a lined baking tray, drizzle olive oil, and massage with black pepper.
4. Roast for 12–15 minutes until bacon is crisp and asparagus tender. Serve warm.

MINI TUNA & CAULIFLOWER PATTIES

PREP TIME

10 MINS

COOK TIME

12 MINS

SERVINGS

3

NUTRITIONAL VALUES (PER SERVING):

Calories: 140 | Fat: 5g | Cholesterol: 65mg | Carbs: 2g | Sugar: 0g | Protein: 18g | Sodium: 320mg

Refrigeration:
Keep up to 3 days.

Reheating:
Warm in skillet or toaster oven.

INGREDIENTS

- 1 cup canned tuna, drained
- 1 cup grated cauliflower
- 1 egg
- 2 tbsp grated Parmesan
- Salt & pepper (to taste)

INSTRUCTIONS

1. Mix tuna, cauliflower, egg, Parmesan, salt, and pepper in a bowl.
2. Form into 6 small patties and place on a greased baking tray.
3. Bake at 375°F for 12 minutes, flipping halfway until golden.
4. Serve hot with a side of lemon or yogurt dip.

BAKED TOFU GARLIC FRIES

PREP TIME

10 MINS

COOK TIME

20 MINS

SERVINGS

2

INGREDIENTS

- 200g firm tofu
- 1 tbsp olive oil
- 1 garlic clove, minced
- Paprika & pepper (to taste)

NUTRITIONAL VALUES (PER SERVING):

Calories: 180 | Fat: 14g | Cholesterol: 0mg | Carbs: 3g | Sugar: 0g | Protein: 13g | Sodium: 15mg

Refrigeration:
Up to 3 days.

Reheating:
Air fry or oven for crispiness.

INSTRUCTIONS

1. Preheat oven to 400°F. Cut tofu into fry-sized sticks and pat dry.
2. Toss with olive oil, minced garlic, paprika, and pepper.
3. Arrange on a baking sheet and bake for 20 min, flipping halfway.
4. Serve with low-carb dipping sauce.

KALE CHIPS WITH CRISPY SALMON FLAKES

PREP TIME

10 MINS

COOK TIME

15 MINS

SERVINGS

2

NUTRITIONAL VALUES (PER SERVING):

Calories: 165 | Fat: 11g | Cholesterol: 30mg | Carbs: 2g | Sugar: 0g | Protein: 14g | Sodium: 180mg

Refrigeration:
Store cooked squash for 2 days.

Reheating:
Best served fresh.

INGREDIENTS

- 2 cups kale leaves, stems removed
- 1 tbsp olive oil
- ½ cup cooked salmon, flaked
- Sea salt & black pepper (to taste)

INSTRUCTIONS

1. Preheat oven to 350°F (175°C). Tear kale into bite-size pieces.
2. In a bowl, massage kale with olive oil and a pinch of salt.
3. Spread kale on a baking sheet and bake for 10 minutes.
4. Toss salmon flakes on top and bake 5 more minutes until kale is crisp and salmon slightly crisped.
5. Serve warm as a crunchy, savory side.

EGG & CHEESE SPINACH CUPS

PREP TIME
05 MINS

COOK TIME
20 MINS

SERVINGS
2

INGREDIENTS

- 4 eggs
- 1 cup spinach, chopped
- ¼ cup shredded mozzarella
- Salt & pepper (to taste)

NUTRITIONAL VALUES (PER SERVING):

Calories: 200 | Fat: 13g | Cholesterol: 375mg | Carbs: 2g | Sugar: 0g | Protein: 18g | Sodium: 220mg

Refrigeration:
Store for up to 3 days.

Reheating:
Reheat in microwave or toaster oven.

INSTRUCTIONS

1. Preheat oven to 375°F (190°C). Grease a muffin tin.
2. Whisk eggs in a bowl, toss in spinach and mozzarella, massage with salt and pepper.
3. Pour into 4 muffin cups and bake for 18–20 minutes until firm.
4. Let cool slightly before removing and serve warm.

LAMB & HERB MEATBALL POPPERS

PREP TIME

10 MINS

COOK TIME

15 MINS

SERVINGS

3

INGREDIENTS

- 300g ground lamb
- 1 tbsp fresh parsley, chopped
- 1 garlic clove, minced
- 1 egg
- Cumin, salt, and pepper (to taste)

NUTRITIONAL VALUES (PER SERVING):

Calories: 230 | Fat: 17g | Cholesterol: 85mg | Carbs: 1g | Sugar: 0g | Protein: 18g | Sodium: 190mg

Refrigeration:
Store up to 3 days in an airtight container.

Reheating:
Reheat in skillet or microwave.

INSTRUCTIONS

1. Preheat oven to 375°F (190°C). Line a baking tray.
2. In a bowl, mix lamb, parsley, garlic, egg, and seasonings.
3. Roll into small meatballs (about 12) and place on tray.
4. Bake for 15 minutes until browned and cooked through.
5. Serve warm with yogurt dip or as-is.

SHRIMP-STUFFED AVOCADO HALVES

PREP TIME
05 MINS

COOK TIME
00 MINS

SERVINGS
2

INGREDIENTS

- 1 ripe avocado, halved and pitted
- ½ cup cooked shrimp, chopped
- 2 tbsp Greek yogurt
- ½ tsp lemon juice
- Paprika & black pepper (to taste)

INSTRUCTIONS

1. In a bowl, mix shrimp with yogurt, lemon juice, paprika, and pepper.
2. Scoop a little avocado flesh out to make more room, then fill each half with the shrimp mixture.
3. Sprinkle a touch of paprika on top and serve immediately.

NUTRITIONAL VALUES (PER SERVING):

Calories: 210 | Fat: 14g | Cholesterol: 95mg | Carbs: 5g | Sugar: 1g | Protein: 15g | Sodium: 150mg

Refrigeration:
Best served fresh.

Reheating:
Not recommended.

COTTAGE CHEESE & HERB-STUFFED TOMATOES

PREP TIME

10 MINS

COOK TIME

00 MINS

SERVINGS

1

NUTRITIONAL VALUES (PER SERVING):

Calories: 145 | Fat: 4g | Cholesterol: 15mg | Carbs: 5g | Sugar: 3g | Protein: 18g | Sodium: 240mg

Refrigeration:
Store for up to 2 days.

Reheating:
Best served cold.

INGREDIENTS

- 2 large tomatoes, tops cut off and centers scooped
- 1 cup low-fat cottage cheese
- 1 tbsp chopped fresh dill or parsley
- Salt & pepper (to taste)

INSTRUCTIONS

1. Mix cottage cheese with herbs, salt, and pepper in a bowl.
2. Stuff each hollowed tomato with the mixture until full.
3. Garnish with extra herbs and serve chilled.

CHICKEN BACON CABBAGE HASH

PREP TIME
05 MINS

COOK TIME
08 MINS

SERVINGS
1

INGREDIENTS

- 1 cup shredded cooked chicken
- 2 turkey bacon strips, chopped
- 2 cups shredded cabbage
- 1 tbsp olive oil
- Garlic powder & black pepper (to taste)

NUTRITIONAL VALUES (PER SERVING):

Calories: 190 | Fat: 10g | Cholesterol: 40mg | Carbs: 3g | Sugar: 1g | Protein: 20g | Sodium: 280mg

Refrigeration:
Store up to 3 days.

Reheating:
Reheat in skillet or microwave.

INSTRUCTIONS

1. Heat oil in a skillet on moderate heat. Sauté bacon for 2–3 minutes.
2. Add cabbage and cook for 5 minutes until wilted.
3. Toss in chicken and seasonings. Stir and cook more for 5–7 minutes until heated through.
4. Serve hot as a savory protein-rich side.

PARMESAN-CRUSTED CHICKEN STRIPS

PREP TIME
10 MINS

COOK TIME
15 MINS

SERVINGS
2

INGREDIENTS

- 2 boneless, skinless chicken breasts, cut into strips
- 1 egg
- ½ cup grated parmesan cheese
- ½ tsp garlic powder
- ½ tsp dried oregano
- Salt & black pepper (to taste)

NUTRITIONAL VALUES (PER SERVING):

Calories: 298 | Fat: 15g | Cholesterol: 140mg | Carbohydrates: 2g | Sugar: 0g | Protein: 37g | Sodium: 428mg | Fiber: 0g

Refrigeration:
Store in an airtight container for 2 day.

Reheating:
Reheat in oven or air fryer at 350°F (175°C) until warm and crispy.

INSTRUCTIONS

1. Preheat oven to 400°F (200°C) and line a baking sheet with parchment paper.
2. Crack the egg into a bowl and whisk until smooth.
3. In another bowl, combine grated parmesan, garlic powder, oregano, salt, and pepper.
4. Dip each chicken strip into the egg, then coat fully in the parmesan mixture.
5. Arrange the strips on the prepared baking sheet in a single layer.
6. Bake for 12–15 minutes or until golden and the chicken is fully cooked through. Flip halfway for even crisping.

DRINKS

CHOCOLATE PEANUT BUTTER PROTEIN SHAKE

PREP TIME

03 MINS

COOK TIME

00 MINS

SERVINGS

1

INGREDIENTS

- 1 cup unsweetened almond milk
- 1 scoop chocolate protein powder
- 1 tbsp unsweetened peanut butter (for nut-free, use sunflower seed butter)

NUTRITIONAL VALUES (PER SERVING):

Calories: 250 | Fat: 13g | Cholesterol: 45mg | Total Carbohydrates: 8g | Sugar: 3g | Protein: 30g | Sodium: 400mg | Fiber: 2.6g

Refrigeration:
Store for up to 12 hours; shake before drinking.

Reheating:
Not applicable.

INSTRUCTIONS

1. Add the almond milk, chocolate protein powder, and peanut butter to a high-speed blender.
2. Blend for 35–40 seconds until smooth and creamy, making sure everything is well combined.
3. For a thicker texture, toss in a few ice cubes and blend again. Pour into a glass and serve cold.

VANILLA ALMOND SMOOTHIE

PREP TIME

03 MINS

COOK TIME

00 MINS

SERVINGS

1

INGREDIENTS

- 1 cup unsweetened almond milk
- 1 scoop vanilla protein powder
- 1 tbsp almond butter (for nut-free, use sunflower seed butter)

NUTRITIONAL VALUES (PER SERVING):

Calories: 248 | Fat: 13.5g | Cholesterol: 40mg | Total Carbohydrates: 7.4g | Sugar: 2g | Protein: 28.4g | Sodium: 320mg | Fiber: 3.2g

Refrigeration:
Store for up to 1 day; shake well before drinking.

Reheating:
Not suitable.

INSTRUCTIONS

1. Pour the almond milk into the food blender, then add the vanilla protein powder and almond butter.
2. Blend on high speed for 30 seconds until creamy and fully combined.
3. Add a few ice cubes for extra chill, blend again briefly, then serve immediately.

MATCHA COCONUT PROTEIN SHAKE

PREP TIME
03 MINS

COOK TIME
00 MINS

SERVINGS
1

INGREDIENTS

- 1 cup unsweetened coconut milk
- 1 scoop vanilla protein powder
- 1 tsp matcha powder

NUTRITIONAL VALUES (PER SERVING):

Calories: 168 | Fat: 6.5g | Cholesterol: 40mg | Total Carbohydrates: 5.4g | Sugar: 1g | Protein: 24.8g | Sodium: 165mg | Fiber: 1.8g

Refrigeration:
Store in the fridge for up to 12 hours.

Reheating:
Not applicable.

INSTRUCTIONS

1. Add the coconut milk, protein powder, and matcha powder to a blender.
2. Blend until smooth and slightly frothy, about 30 seconds.
3. Serve immediately over ice or chilled for a refreshing, energizing drink.

STRAWBERRY COLLAGEN SMOOTHIE

PREP TIME

03 MINS

COOK TIME

00 MINS

SERVINGS

1

NUTRITIONAL VALUES (PER SERVING):

Calories: 215 | Fat: 4.7g | Cholesterol: 40mg | Total Carbohydrates: 10g | Sugar: 4.5g | Protein: 35.5g | Sodium: 340mg | Fiber: 2.9g

Refrigeration:
Store in an air-sealed container for up to 24 hours.

Reheating:
Not recommended.

INGREDIENTS

- 1 cup unsweetened almond milk
- ½ cup fresh or frozen strawberries
- 1 scoop collagen powder
- 1 scoop vanilla protein powder

INSTRUCTIONS

1. Place all ingredients into the powerful blender jar.
2. Blend on full power for 30–45 seconds until smooth and creamy.
3. Pour into a glass and enjoy cold—add ice if you prefer a thicker texture.

CINNAMON COFFEE SHAKE

PREP TIME
03 MINS

COOK TIME
00 MINS

SERVINGS
1

NUTRITIONAL VALUES (PER SERVING):

Calories: 139 | Fat: 3.35g | Cholesterol: 40mg | Total Carbohydrates: 4.3g | Sugar: 1g | Protein: 24.8g | Sodium: 240mg | Fiber: 1.8g

Refrigeration:
Store for up to 8 hours in the fridge.

Reheating:
Not suitable for heating.

INGREDIENTS

- ½ cup cold brew coffee
- ½ cup unsweetened almond milk
- 1 scoop vanilla protein powder
- ½ tsp ground cinnamon

INSTRUCTIONS

1. In a powerful food blender, combine coffee, almond milk, protein powder, and cinnamon.
2. Blend for 30 seconds until fully mixed and slightly frothy.
3. Serve cold, over ice if desired, for a smooth energy boost.

KETO GREEN SUPERFOOD SMOOTHIE

PREP TIME

03 MINS

COOK TIME

00 MINS

SERVINGS

1

INGREDIENTS

- 1 cup unsweetened almond milk
- 1 scoop vanilla protein powder
- 1 cup fresh spinach

NUTRITIONAL VALUES (PER SERVING):

Calories: 157 | Fat: 4.6g | Cholesterol: 40mg | Total Carbohydrates: 5.1g | Sugar: 1.1g | Protein: 25.9g | Sodium: 344mg | Fiber: 2.3g

Refrigeration:
Store for up to 12 hours. Shake well before serving.

Reheating:
Not applicable.

INSTRUCTIONS

1. Add almond milk, protein powder, and spinach to a high-speed blender.
2. Blend for 30–45 seconds until smooth and well combined.
3. Serve chilled or over ice pieces for a refreshing, nutrient-rich drink.

AVOCADO & MINT SHAKE

PREP TIME
04 MINS

COOK TIME
00 MINS

SERVINGS
1

INGREDIENTS

- 1 cup unsweetened almond milk
- 1 scoop vanilla protein powder
- ½ medium avocado
- 1 tbsp fresh mint leaves

NUTRITIONAL VALUES (PER SERVING):

Calories: 271 | Fat: 15.5g | Cholesterol: 40mg | Total Carbohydrates: 10.2g | Sugar: 1.2g | Protein: 26.6g | Sodium: 325mg | Fiber: 6.7g

Refrigeration:
Store for up to 1 day. Shake before drinking.

Reheating:
Not applicable.

INSTRUCTIONS

1. Blend almond milk, protein powder, avocado, and mint leaves until creamy and thick.
2. Add ice pieces and blend again for a chilled, smooth texture.
3. Pour into a tall glass and spread with a mint leaf if desired.

ICED CHIA ALMOND LATTE

PREP TIME

03 MINS

COOK TIME

00 MINS

SERVINGS

1

INGREDIENTS

- ½ cup cold brew coffee
- ½ cup unsweetened almond milk
- 1 scoop vanilla protein powder
- 1 tbsp chia seeds

NUTRITIONAL VALUES (PER SERVING):

Calories: 194 | Fat: 7g | Cholesterol: 40mg | Total Carbohydrates: 8.5g | Sugar: 1g | Protein: 26.8g | Sodium: 241mg | Fiber: 5.4g

Refrigeration:
Store for up to 8 hours. Shake or stir before use.

Reheating:
Not recommended.

INSTRUCTIONS

1. Combine cold brew, almond milk, protein powder, and chia seeds into the food blender.
2. Blend on full power for 30 seconds, then let sit for 1–2 minutes so the chia begins to swell.
3. Serve over ice for a creamy and energizing boost.

TURMERIC VANILLA SMOOTHIE

PREP TIME

03 MINS

COOK TIME

00 MINS

SERVINGS

1

INGREDIENTS

- 1 cup unsweetened coconut milk
- 1 scoop vanilla protein powder
- ½ tsp turmeric powder

NUTRITIONAL VALUES (PER SERVING):

Calories: 169 | Fat: 6.6g | Cholesterol: 40mg | Total Carbohydrates: 5.7g | Sugar: 1g | Protein: 24.6g | Sodium: 165mg | Fiber: 1.7g

Refrigeration:
Best consumed fresh or within 12 hours.

Reheating:
Not applicable.

INSTRUCTIONS

1. In a powerful food blender, mix coconut milk, protein powder, and turmeric until fully blended.
2. Add ice if preferred and blend again for a smooth, golden shake.
3. Serve immediately with a pinch of cinnamon or black pepper on top (optional).

COCONUT ESPRESSO PROTEIN DRINK

PREP TIME
02 MINS

COOK TIME
00 MINS

SERVINGS
1

NUTRITIONAL VALUES (PER SERVING):

Calories: 166 | Fat: 6.5g | Cholesterol: 40mg | Total Carbohydrates: 5g | Sugar: 1g | Protein: 24.6g | Sodium: 170mg | Fiber: 1.5g

Refrigeration:
Store for up to 1 day. Shake before serving.

Reheating:
Not suitable.

INGREDIENTS

- 1 shot espresso
- 1 cup unsweetened coconut milk
- 1 scoop vanilla protein powder

INSTRUCTIONS

1. Combine hot or cooled espresso with coconut milk and protein powder in a shaker or blender.
2. Shake it thoroughly and properly until smooth and frothy.
3. Serve over ice or drink immediately for a protein-packed energy boost.

DESSERTS

CHOCOLATE AVOCADO MOUSSE

PREP TIME

05 MINS

COOK TIME

00 MINS

SERVINGS

2

INGREDIENTS

- ½ medium avocado
- 1 tbsp unsweetened cocoa powder
- 1 scoop vanilla protein powder

NUTRITIONAL VALUES (PER SERVING):

Calories: 210 | Fat: 18g | Cholesterol: 0mg | Total Carbohydrates: 6g | Sugar: 2.5g | Protein: 6g | Sodium: 40mg | Fiber: 3g

Refrigeration:
Store covered for up to 24 hours.

Reheating:
Not needed.

INSTRUCTIONS

1. Scoop the avocado into a food blender and add cocoa powder and protein powder.
2. Blend until its texture turns smooth and creamy, scraping down the sides as needed to avoid lumps.
3. Chill for 10–15 minutes before serving for a firmer texture.

KETO CHEESECAKE FAT BOMBS

PREP TIME
10 MINS

COOK TIME
00 MINS

SERVINGS
6

NUTRITIONAL VALUES (PER SERVING):

Calories: 120 | Fat: 11g | Cholesterol: 15mg | Total Carbohydrates: 2g | Sugar: 0.6g | Protein: 3g | Sodium: 35mg | Fiber: 0.5g

Refrigeration:
Store in an air-sealed container for up to 3 days.

Reheating:
Not applicable.

INGREDIENTS

- 2 tbsp cream cheese (use lactose-free if needed)
- 1 scoop vanilla protein powder
- 2 tbsp shredded coconut

INSTRUCTIONS

1. Grab the shallow bowl and mix softened cream cheese and protein powder until smooth and well combined.
2. Roll the mixture into bite-sized balls (about ping pong ball size) and coat them with shredded coconut.
3. Place on a parchment-lined tray and refrigerate for 30 minutes (at least) before serving.

PEANUT BUTTER PROTEIN BALLS

PREP TIME
05 MINS

COOK TIME
00 MINS

SERVINGS
6

INGREDIENTS

- 1 tbsp peanut butter (for nut-free, use sunflower seed butter)
- 1 scoop vanilla protein powder
- 2 tbsp shredded coconut

NUTRITIONAL VALUES (PER SERVING):

Calories: 145 | Fat: 12g | Cholesterol: 0mg | Total Carbohydrates: 3g | Sugar: 1.2g | Protein: 7g | Sodium: 60mg | Fiber: 1g

Refrigeration:
Best stored in the fridge for up to 3 days.

Reheating:
Not needed.

INSTRUCTIONS

1. Grab the shallow bowl and mix peanut butter with protein powder. Mix them thoroughly until it forms a thick dough.
2. Add shredded coconut and roll into small round balls.
3. Let them chill in the fridge for 20–30 minutes to firm up before serving.

LEMON COCONUT CREAM CUPS

PREP TIME
5 MINS

COOK TIME
00 MINS

SERVINGS
4

INGREDIENTS

- 1 tbsp lemon juice
- 1 scoop vanilla protein powder
- 2 tbsp shredded coconut
- 2 tbsp cream cheese (use dairy-free cream cheese if needed)

NUTRITIONAL VALUES (PER SERVING):

Calories: 160 | Fat: 14g | Cholesterol: 5mg | Total Carbohydrates: 4g | Sugar: 1g | Protein: 4g | Sodium: 20mg | Fiber: 1.2g

Refrigeration:
Store covered for up to 3 days.

Reheating:
Not applicable.

INSTRUCTIONS

1. Blend the cream cheese, lemon juice, and protein powder in a small bowl until smooth.
2. Stir in the shredded coconut and mix properly until well combined.
3. Spoon into small dessert cups and chill for at least 15 minutes before serving.

CHIA ALMOND PUDDING

PREP TIME

05 MINS

COOK TIME

00 MINS

SERVINGS

2

INGREDIENTS

- 1 tbsp chia seeds
- 1 scoop vanilla protein powder
- ½ cup unsweetened almond milk

NUTRITIONAL VALUES (PER SERVING):

Calories: 185 | Fat: 14g | Cholesterol: 0mg | Total Carbohydrates: 6g | Sugar: 1.5g | Protein: 8g | Sodium: 35mg | Fiber: 5g

Refrigeration:
Store for up to 3 days in a sealed jar.

Reheating:
Serve cold only.

INSTRUCTIONS

1. Combine chia seeds, almond milk, and protein powder in a mixing jar.
2. Stir well, cover, and chill for 1 hour (at least) or overnight for best consistency.
3. Stir again before serving, and top with a few almond slices if desired.

LOW-CARB VANILLA ICE CREAM

PREP TIME
5 MINS

COOK TIME
00 MINS

SERVINGS
4

INGREDIENTS

- ¼ cup heavy cream
- 1 scoop vanilla protein powder

NUTRITIONAL VALUES (PER SERVING):

Calories: 170 | Fat: 15g | Cholesterol: 50mg | Total Carbohydrates: 3g | Sugar: 1.2g | Protein: 6g | Sodium: 40mg | Fiber: 0g

Refrigeration:
Store frozen for up to 3 days.

Reheating:
Not applicable—allow to thaw slightly before serving.

INSTRUCTIONS

1. smooth and slightly thickened.
2. Pour into a freezer-safe container and freeze for at least 2–3 hours until set. Stir once after an hour to avoid icy texture.
3. Let sit at room temperature for a couple of minutes before scooping and serving.

STRAWBERRY COCONUT CREAM BITES

PREP TIME

05 MINS

COOK TIME

00 MINS

SERVINGS

6

INGREDIENTS

- 2 medium strawberries, finely chopped
- 1 scoop vanilla protein powder
- 2 tbsp shredded coconut

NUTRITIONAL VALUES (PER SERVING):

Calories: 110 | Fat: 9g | Cholesterol: 0mg | Total Carbohydrates: 4g | Sugar: 2g | Protein: 2g | Sodium: 15mg | Fiber: 1g

Refrigeration:
Store in an airtight container in the refrigerator for up to 3 days.

Reheating:
Not applicable.

INSTRUCTIONS

1. In a small, deep-bottom bowl, mash the strawberries and mix them with protein powder to form a soft dough.
2. Add shredded coconut and stir until well combined, then press into small bite-sized molds or roll into balls.
3. Chill for 15–20 minutes (in the fridge not freezer) before serving to firm them up.

DARK CHOCOLATE WALNUT CLUSTERS

PREP TIME

5 MINS

COOK TIME

00 MINS

SERVINGS

6

INGREDIENTS

- 1 tbsp dark chocolate chips
- 1 scoop vanilla protein powder
- 2 tbsp chopped walnuts

NUTRITIONAL VALUES (PER SERVING):

Calories: 140 | Fat: 12g | Cholesterol: 0mg | Total Carbohydrates: 5g | Sugar: 2g | Protein: 3g | Sodium: 5mg | Fiber: 2g

Refrigeration:
Store in an airtight container in the refrigerator for up to 3 days.

Reheating:
Not required.

INSTRUCTIONS

1. Melt chocolate chips gently in a microwave-safe bowl for 15–20 seconds.
2. Stir in protein powder and walnuts until evenly coated and clumpy.
3. Drop spoonfuls onto the parchment paper-arranged tray and refrigerate until firm, about 20 minutes.

KETO RICOTTA MOUSSE

PREP TIME
05 MINS

COOK TIME
00 MINS

SERVINGS
2

INGREDIENTS

- ¼ cup ricotta cheese
- 1 scoop vanilla protein powder
- ¼ cup heavy cream

NUTRITIONAL VALUES (PER SERVING):

Calories: 190 | Fat: 16g | Cholesterol: 30mg | Total Carbohydrates: 3g | Sugar: 1g | Protein: 8g | Sodium: 50mg | Fiber: 0g

Refrigeration:
Store in an airtight container in the refrigerator for up to 3 days.

Reheating:
Not applicable.

INSTRUCTIONS

1. Take the medium shallow bowl, whip together the ricotta, heavy cream, and protein powder until fluffy and smooth.
2. Spoon the mousse into the wide-mouth serving bowl and chill for at least 20 minutes before enjoying it.
3. Optional: sprinkle cinnamon powder or cocoa powder on top before serving.

ALMOND BUTTER FUDGE SQUARES

PREP TIME

5 MINS

COOK TIME

00 MINS

SERVINGS

6

INGREDIENTS

- 2 tbsp almond butter
- 1 scoop vanilla protein powder
- 2 tbsp shredded coconut

NUTRITIONAL VALUES (PER SERVING):

Calories: 160 | Fat: 14g | Cholesterol: 0mg | Total Carbohydrates: 3g | Sugar: 1.2g | Protein: 5g | Sodium: 45mg | Fiber: 1g

Refrigeration:
Store in an airtight container in the refrigerator for up to 3 days.

Reheating:
Not needed.

INSTRUCTIONS

1. Mix almond butter and protein powder in a deep-bottom bowl until thick and dough-like.
2. Fold in the shredded coconut, then press the mixture into a silicone mold or small square dish.
3. Freeze for 20 minutes or until firm, then slice into squares and enjoy.

30 DAY MEAL PLAN AND SHOPPING LIST

WEEK 1

	BREAKFAST	LUNCH	DINNER	SNACK	MACROS
DAY 1	Cheesy Scrambled Eggs with Smoked Salmon (page 9)	Stuffed Bell Peppers with Ground Turkey (page 30)	Lemon Garlic Butter Chicken (page 41)	Bacon-Wrapped Asparagus Bundles (page 73)	**Calories: 1120 | Protein: 85g | Carbs: 10g | Fat: 80g**
DAY 2	Keto Cottage Cheese Pancakes (page 10)	Spinach Chicken Bowl with Feta (page 31)	Herb-Crusted Salmon (page 42)	Mini Tuna & Cauliflower Patties (page 74)	**Calories: 1085 | Protein: 86g | Carbs: 11g | Fat: 74g**
DAY 3	Ground Turkey & Egg Scramble (page 11)	Broccoli & Bacon Salad (page 32)	Garlic Herb Lamb Chops (page 43)	Baked Tofu Garlic Fries (page 75)	**Calories: 1176 | Protein: 79g | Carbs: 12g | Fat: 93g**
DAY 4	Low-Carb Sausage Muffins (page 12)	Avocado Chicken Salad (page 33)	Stuffed Chicken Breast with Cream Cheese (page 44)	Kale Chips with Crispy Salmon Flakes (page 76)	**Calories: 1165 | Protein: 91g | Carbs: 9g | Fat: 83g**
DAY 5	Protein Chia Pudding with Almond Butter & Whey (page 13)	Crispy Tofu & Cabbage Slaw (page 34)	Keto Beef Stir-Fry (page 45)	Egg & Cheese Spinach Cups (page 77)	**Calories: 1100 | Protein: 81g | Carbs: 19g | Fat: 75g**
DAY 6	Spinach & Feta Egg Scramble (page 14)	Smoked Salmon & Egg Salad (page 35)	Baked Cod with Lemon & Olive Oil (page 46)	Lamb & Herb Meatball Poppers (page 78)	**Calories: 1020 | Protein: 75g | Carbs: 12g | Fat: 72g**
DAY 7	Savory Tofu Scramble (page 15)	Tuna Egg Stuffed Tomatoes (page 36)	Keto Pork Chops with Herbs (page 47)	Shrimp-Stuffed Avocado Halves (page 79)	**Calories: 1072 | Protein: 83g | Carbs: 14g | Fat: 76g**

WEEK 2

	BREAKFAST	LUNCH	DINNER	SNACK	MACROS
DAY 1	Keto Greek Yogurt Parfait (page 16)	Cauliflower Tabbouleh with Chicken (page 37)	Shrimp Skewers with Garlic Marinade (page 48)	Peanut Butter Protein Balls (page 97)	**Calories: 1095 | Protein: 87g | Carbs: 13g | Fat: 76g**
DAY 2	Flaxseed Protein Smoothie (page 17)	Tuna Nori Seaweed Wraps (page 38)	Keto Lamb Burgers (page 49)	Keto Cheesecake Fat Bombs (page 96)	**Calories: 1065 | Protein: 83g | Carbs: 10g | Fat: 74g**
DAY 3	Cauliflower Hash Brown & Egg Stack (page 18)	Chili Lime Shrimp & Cauliflower Rice Bowl (page 39)	Zucchini Lasagna with Ground Turkey (page 50)	Chocolate Avocado Mousse (page 95)	**Calories: 1140 | Protein: 88g | Carbs: 14g | Fat: 81g**
DAY 4	Almond Butter Protein Muffins (page 19)	Stuffed Bell Peppers with Ground Turkey (page 30)	Baked Chicken Drumsticks with Paprika (page 51)	Low-Carb Vanilla Ice Cream (page 100)	**Calories: 1170 | Protein: 90g | Carbs: 11g | Fat: 85g**
DAY 5	Zucchini & Egg Frittata (page 20)	Spinach Chicken Bowl with Feta (page 31)	Keto Chicken Alfredo (page 52)	Chia Almond Pudding (page 99)	**Calories: 1115 | Protein: 86g | Carbs: 10g | Fat: 78g**
DAY 6	Turkey Bacon Egg Cups (page 21)	Broccoli & Bacon Salad (page 32)	Steak with Mushroom Sauce (page 53)	Dark Chocolate Walnut Clusters (page 102)	**Calories: 1135 | Protein: 84g | Carbs: 13g | Fat: 82g**
DAY 7	Keto Chia Yogurt Bowl (page 22)	Avocado Chicken Salad (page 33)	Spicy Grilled Shrimp with Herbs (page 54)	Almond Butter Fudge Squares (page 104)	**Calories: 1088 | Protein: 80g | Carbs: 11g | Fat: 78g**

WEEK 3

	BREAKFAST	LUNCH	DINNER	SNACK	MACROS
DAY 1	Scrambled Eggs with Pesto (page 23)	Tuna Egg Stuffed Tomatoes (page 36)	Turkey Patties with Creamy Spinach (page 55)	Peanut Butter Protein Balls (page 97)	**Calories: 1120 | Protein: 87g | Carbs: 11g | Fat: 80g**
DAY 2	Vanilla Almond Protein Shake (page 24)	Cauliflower Tabbouleh with Chicken (page 37)	Lemon Garlic Butter Chicken (page 41)	Keto Cheesecake Fat Bombs (page 96)	**Calories: 1098 | Protein: 85g | Carbs: 10g | Fat: 77g**
DAY 3	Savory Tofu Breakfast Wrap (page 25)	Tuna Nori Seaweed Wraps (page 38)	Herb-Crusted Salmon (page 42)	Chocolate Avocado Mousse (page 95)	**Calories: 1125 | Protein: 83g | Carbs: 14g | Fat: 79g**
DAY 4	Mushroom & Herb Omelet (page 26)	Chili Lime Shrimp & Cauliflower Rice Bowl (page 39)	Garlic Herb Lamb Chops (page 43)	Low-Carb Vanilla Ice Cream (page 100)	**Calories: 1140 | Protein: 89g | Carbs: 10g | Fat: 83g**
DAY 5	Coconut Cream Chia Bowl (page 27)	Stuffed Bell Peppers with Ground Turkey (page 30)	Stuffed Chicken Breast with Cream Cheese (page 44)	Chia Almond Pudding (page 99)	**Calories: 1130 | Protein: 86g | Carbs: 13g | Fat: 80g**
DAY 6	Eggs in Avocado Boats (page 28)	Spinach Chicken Bowl with Feta (page 31)	Keto Beef Stir-Fry (page 45)	Dark Chocolate Walnut Clusters (page 102)	**Calories: 1112 | Protein: 83g | Carbs: 11g | Fat: 81g**
DAY 7	Keto Cottage Cheese Pancakes (page 10)	Broccoli & Bacon Salad (page 32)	Baked Cod with Lemon & Olive Oil (page 46)	Almond Butter Fudge Squares (page 104)	**Calories: 1080 | Protein: 84g | Carbs: 12g | Fat: 76g**

WEEK 4

	BREAKFAST	LUNCH	DINNER	SNACK	MACROS
DAY 1	Ground Turkey & Egg Scramble (page 11)	Avocado Chicken Salad (page 33)	Keto Pork Chops with Herbs (page 47)	Peanut Butter Protein Balls (page 97)	**Calories: 1132 | Protein: 88g | Carbs: 9g | Fat: 82g**
DAY 2	Protein Chia Pudding with Almond Butter & Whey (page 13)	Crispy Tofu & Cabbage Slaw (page 34)	Shrimp Skewers with Garlic Marinade (page 48)	Keto Cheesecake Fat Bombs (page 96)	**Calories: 1110 | Protein: 84g | Carbs: 11g | Fat: 77g**
DAY 3	Spinach & Feta Egg Scramble (page 14)	Smoked Salmon & Egg Salad (page 35)	Keto Lamb Burgers (page 49)	Chocolate Avocado Mousse (page 95)	**Calories: 1100 | Protein: 81g | Carbs: 12g | Fat: 78g**
DAY 4	Savory Tofu Scramble (page 15)	Tuna Egg Stuffed Tomatoes (page 36)	Zucchini Lasagna with Ground Turkey (page 50)	Low-Carb Vanilla Ice Cream (page 100)	**Calories: 1125 | Protein: 86g | Carbs: 11g | Fat: 80g**
DAY 5	Keto Greek Yogurt Parfait (page 16)	Cauliflower Tabbouleh with Chicken (page 37)	Baked Chicken Drumsticks with Paprika (page 51)	Chia Almond Pudding (page 99)	**Calories: 1095 | Protein: 83g | Carbs: 13g | Fat: 76g**
DAY 6	Flaxseed Protein Smoothie (page 17)	Tuna Nori Seaweed Wraps (page 38)	Keto Chicken Alfredo (page 52)	Dark Chocolate Walnut Clusters (page 102)	**Calories: 1108 | Protein: 84g | Carbs: 11g | Fat: 78g**
DAY 7	Cauliflower Hash Brown & Egg Stack (page 18)	Chili Lime Shrimp & Cauliflower Rice Bowl (page 39)	Steak with Mushroom Sauce (page 53)	Almond Butter Fudge Squares (page 104)	**Calories: 1145 | Protein: 89g | Carbs: 13g | Fat: 82g**
BONUS DAY	Almond Butter Protein Muffins (page 19)	Stuffed Bell Peppers with Ground Turkey (page 30)	Baked Chicken Drumsticks with Paprika (page 51)	Low-Carb Vanilla Ice Cream (page 100)	**Calories: 1170 | Protein: 90g | Carbs: 11g | Fat: 85g**
BONUS DAY	Coconut Cream Chia Bowl (page 27)	Stuffed Bell Peppers with Ground Turkey (page 30)	Stuffed Chicken Breast with Cream Cheese (page 44)	Chia Almond Pudding (page 99)	**Calories: 1130 | Protein: 86g | Carbs: 13g | Fat: 80g**

Week 1 Shopping List

Proteins – Dairy-Free

- [ ] 6 skinless chicken breasts
- [ ] 1 pack ground turkey (500g)
- [ ] 2 cod fillets
- [ ] 2 salmon fillets
- [ ] 1 pack smoked salmon
- [ ] 1 steak (sirloin or ribeye)
- [ ] 1 pack shrimp (300g)
- [ ] 1 block firm tofu
- [ ] 1 dozen eggs
- [ ] 1 tub vanilla protein powder
- [ ] Proteins – Dairy
- [ ] 1 cup cottage cheese
- [ ] 2 cups Greek yogurt
- [ ] 1 pack cream cheese
- [ ] 1 cup shredded cheddar cheese
- [ ] ½ cup grated Parmesan cheese
- [ ] ¼ cup heavy cream
- [ ] 1 stick butter

Vegetables

- [ ] 6 cups spinach
- [ ] 3 medium zucchinis
- [ ] 2 large cucumbers
- [ ] 1 small cabbage
- [ ] 2 tomatoes
- [ ] 2 bell peppers
- [ ] 2 cups broccoli florets
- [ ] 1 head cauliflower
- [ ] 1 bunch asparagus
- [ ] 1 cup mushrooms
- [ ] 1 head romaine lettuce
- [ ] 1 bunch parsley
- [ ] 2 lemons
- [ ] 1 garlic bulb

Fruits

- [ ] 1 cup mixed berries
- [ ] 2 avocados

Nuts & Seeds

- [ ] Chopped walnuts
- [ ] Flaxseeds
- [ ] Chia seeds
- [ ] Shredded coconut
- [ ] Almond butter
- [ ] Peanut butter

Other Essentials (Dairy-Free)

- [ ] Olive oil
- [ ] Apple cider vinegar
- [ ] Mustard
- [ ] Soy sauce
- [ ] Baking powder
- [ ] Pesto
- [ ] Tomato paste
- [ ] Almond milk
- [ ] Coconut milk

Week 2 Shopping List

Proteins – Dairy-Free

- [ ] 6 skinless chicken breasts
- [ ] 1 pack ground turkey (500g)
- [ ] 1 steak (sirloin)
- [ ] 1 pack shrimp
- [ ] 1 can tuna
- [ ] 1 block tofu
- [ ] 1 dozen eggs
- [ ] 1 tub vanilla protein powder

Proteins – Dairy

- [ ] 1 pack cream cheese
- [ ] 1 cup shredded cheddar cheese
- [ ] ½ cup grated Parmesan cheese
- [ ] 1 cup cottage cheese
- [ ] 1 cup Greek yogurt
- [ ] 1 stick butter
- [ ] ¼ cup heavy cream

Vegetables

- [ ] 4 cups spinach
- [ ] 2 zucchinis
- [ ] 2 bell peppers
- [ ] 2 tomatoes
- [ ] 1 head lettuce
- [ ] 1 head cauliflower
- [ ] 2 avocados
- [ ] 1 bunch parsley
- [ ] 1 lemon
- [ ] 1 garlic bulb
- [ ] 1 small cabbage
- [ ] 1 cucumber
- [ ] 2 cups broccoli
- [ ] 1 small onion

Fruits

- [ ] 1 cup mixed berries
- [ ] 2 avocados
- [ ] 1 lemon
- [ ] Nuts & Seeds
- [ ] Chia seeds
- [ ] Flaxseeds
- [ ] Shredded coconut
- [ ] Almond butter
- [ ] Peanut butter
- [ ] Walnuts

Other Essentials (Dairy-Free)

- [ ] Olive oil
- [ ] Apple cider vinegar
- [ ] Soy sauce
- [ ] Baking powder
- [ ] Almond milk
- [ ] Coconut milk
- [ ] Dark chocolate chips
- [ ] Nori sheets
- [ ] Vanilla protein powder

Week 3 Shopping List

Proteins – Dairy-Free

- [ ] 6 chicken breasts
- [ ] 1 pack ground turkey
- [ ] 2 steaks
- [ ] 1 pack shrimp
- [ ] 1 can tuna
- [ ] 1 dozen eggs
- [ ] 1 block firm tofu
- [ ] 1 tub vanilla protein powder

Proteins – Dairy

- [ ] 1 cup Greek yogurt
- [ ] 1 pack cream cheese
- [ ] ½ cup grated Parmesan
- [ ] 1 cup cheddar cheese
- [ ] 1 stick butter
- [ ] ¼ cup heavy cream

Vegetables

- [ ] 6 cups spinach
- [ ] 2 zucchinis
- [ ] 1 small cauliflower
- [ ] 2 bell peppers
- [ ] 1 head lettuce
- [ ] 1 cucumber
- [ ] 1 garlic bulb
- [ ] 1 lemon
- [ ] 1 tomato
- [ ] 2 avocados
- [ ] 1 head cabbage
- [ ] 1 bunch parsley

1 cup mushrooms

Fruits

- [ ] 1 cup berries
- [ ] 2 avocados
- [ ] 1 lemon
- [ ] Nuts & Seeds
- [ ] Chia seeds
- [ ] Almond butter
- [ ] Peanut butter
- [ ] Walnuts
- [ ] Shredded coconut
- [ ] Flaxseeds

Other Essentials (Dairy-Free)

- [ ] Olive oil
- [ ] Apple cider vinegar
- [ ] Soy sauce
- [ ] Baking powder
- [ ] Coconut milk
- [ ] Almond milk
- [ ] Dark chocolate chips
- [ ] Pesto
- [ ] Tomato paste

Week 4 Shopping List

Proteins – Dairy-Free

- [ ] 6 chicken breasts
- [ ] 1 pack ground turkey
- [ ] 2 salmon fillets
- [ ] 1 steak
- [ ] 1 can tuna
- [ ] 1 dozen eggs
- [ ] 1 block tofu
- [ ] 1 pack shrimp
- [ ] 1 tub vanilla protein powder

Proteins – Dairy

- [ ] 1 pack cream cheese
- [ ] 1 cup cottage cheese
- [ ] 1 cup shredded cheddar
- [ ] ½ cup grated Parmesan
- [ ] 1 stick butter
- [ ] ¼ cup heavy cream
- [ ] 1 cup Greek yogurt

Vegetables

- [ ] 6 cups spinach
- [ ] 2 zucchinis
- [ ] 1 head lettuce
- [ ] 1 small cauliflower
- [ ] 1 cucumber
- [ ] 2 bell peppers
- [ ] 1 tomato
- [ ] 1 lemon
- [ ] 1 garlic bulb
- [ ] 2 avocados
- [ ] 1 cup mushrooms
- [ ] 1 bunch parsley

Fruits

- [ ] 1 cup mixed berries
- [ ] 2 avocados
- [ ] 1 lemon
- [ ] Nuts & Seeds
- [ ] Almond butter
- [ ] Peanut butter
- [ ] Chia seeds
- [ ] Flaxseeds
- [ ] Walnuts
- [ ] Shredded coconut

Other Essentials (Dairy-Free)

- [ ] Olive oil
- [ ] Apple cider vinegar
- [ ] Soy sauce
- [ ] Baking powder
- [ ] Coconut milk
- [ ] Almond milk
- [ ] Nori sheets
- [ ] Dark chocolate chips
- [ ] Pesto
- [ ] Tomato paste

CONCLUSION

Congratulations on reaching the end of your Low-Carb, High-Protein journey! Whether you started this cookbook with the goal of losing weight, boosting your energy, stabilizing blood sugar, or simply eating better, you now have everything you need to continue that journey with confidence.
With quick, 5-ingredient recipes, an easy-to-follow 30-day meal plan, weekly shopping lists, and downloadable resources at your fingertips, healthy eating no longer has to be complicated or overwhelming. Each recipe was thoughtfully created to strike the perfect balance between convenience, flavor, and nutrition, making it easier than ever to stick to your goals without sacrificing enjoyment.

But this book is more than just a collection of meals, it's a guide to building sustainable habits that support long-term health. You've learned how simple ingredients can come together to create high-protein, low-carb dishes that satisfy your appetite, nourish your body, and fuel your day. You've also discovered that eating clean doesn't require restrictive rules, it just requires the right tools and a little inspiration.

As you move forward, don't feel pressured to be perfect. The best results come from consistency, not extremes. Revisit the recipes you loved, experiment with new ones, and trust that every small choice adds up.

Thank you for allowing this cookbook to be part of your lifestyle transformation. If you found this book helpful, inspiring, or just deliciously practical, please consider leaving a review, we'd love to hear about your success!

Here's to feeling stronger, eating smarter, and living better, one high-protein, low-carb meal at a time.

INDEX

Made in the USA
Monee, IL
17 July 2025

15f79618-c40e-41bf-97a7-a6ab3d61af77R01